POWER TALK.

—————— ◆ ——————

Language and Interaction in Institutional Discourse

D0141396

REAL LANGUAGE SERIES

General Editors:

JENNIFER COATES, University of Surrey, Roehampton

JENNY CHESHIRE, Queen Mary and Westfield College, University of London, and

EUAN ERID, Institute of Education, University of London

Titles published in the series:

Norman Fairclough (Editor) Critical Language Awareness

James Milroy and Lesley Milroy (Editors) Real English: The Grammar of English Dialects in the British Isles

Mark Sebba London Jamaican: Language Systems in Interaction

Janet Holmes Women, Men and Politeness

Ben Rampton Crossing: Language and Ethnicity Among Adolescents

Brian V. Street Social Literacies: Critical Approaches to Literacy in Development, Ethnography and Education

Srikant Sarangi and Stefaan Slembrouck Language, Bureaucracy and Social Control

Ruth Wodak Disorders of Discourse

Victoria L. Bergvall, Janet M. Being and Alice F. Freed (Editors) Rethinking Language and Gender Research: Theory and Practice

Anne Pauwels Women Changing Language

Monica Heller Linguistic Minorities and Modernity: A Sociolinguistic Ethnography

Alison Sealey Childly Language: Children, Language and the Soical World

Shelley Angélil-Carter Stolen Language? Plagiarism in Writing

POWER TALK

—◆—

Language and Interaction in Institutional Discourse

Joanna Thornborrow

An imprint of **Pearson Education**

Harlow, England · London · New York · Reading, Massachusetts · San Francisco
Toronto · Don Mills, Ontario · Sydney · Tokyo · Singapore · Hong Kong · Seoul
Taipei · Cape Town · Madrid · Mexico City · Amsterdam · Munich · Paris · Milan

PEARSON EDUCATION LIMITED

Head Office:
Edinburgh Gate
Harlow CM20 2JE
Tel: +44 (0)1279 623623
Fax: +44 (0)1279 431059

London Office:
128 Long Acre
London WC2E 9AN
Tel: +44 (0)20 7447 2000
Fax: +44 (0)20 7240 5771
Website: www.history-minds.com

_____

First published in Great Britain in 2002

© Pearson Education 2002

The right of Joanna Thornborrow to be identified as Author
of this Work has been asserted by her in accordance
with the Copyright, Designs and Patents Act 1988.

ISBN 0 582 36879 0

British Library Cataloguing in Publication Data
A CIP catalogue record for this book can be obtained from the British Library

All rights reserved; no part of this publication may be reproduced, stored
in a retrieval system, or transmitted in any form or by any means, electronic,
mechanical, photocopying, recording, or otherwise without either the prior
written permission of the Publishers or a licence permitting restricted copying
in the United Kingdom issued by the Copyright Licensing Agency Ltd,
90 Tottenham Court Road, London W1P 0LP. This book may not be lent,
resold, hired out or otherwise disposed of by way of trade in any form
of binding or cover other than that in which it is published, without the
prior consent of the Publishers.

10 9 8 7 6 5 4 3 2
07 06 05 04 03

Set in 10.5/12pt Garamond MT by Graphicraft Limited, Hong Kong
Produced by Pearson Education Asia Pte Ltd
Printed in Malaysia, PA

The Publishers' policy is to use paper manufactured from sustainable forests.

For Ian, Alice and Nico

CONTENTS

———— ◆ ————

ACKNOWLEDGEMENTS

———— ◆ ————

Many people have contributed in one way or another to the process of getting this book written. Among some of the most significant in the early stages are former colleagues and friends in the English Language and Linguistics Programme at the University of Surrey Roehampton, who were always available to discuss ideas, talk through problems, and occasionally even look after my children. I would also like to thank my colleagues at the Centre for Language and Communication Research at Cardiff University for their interest and support during the final stages. My special thanks and appreciation go to the following people:

My parents and sisters, for their constant support, and for always providing a space to talk; Jen Coates, for her enthusiasm, encouragement and critical advice throughout the time it has taken to write the book; Linda Thomas, for her continuing friendship through difficult circumstances and out the other side; Martin Montgomery, my PhD supervisor at Strathclyde University, who first introduced me to critical discourse analysis, conversation analysis and the spaces in between; and especially Ian Hutchby, for having been there to argue with.

I am grateful to the British Academy for their funding of my research project on classroom talk, and to the children whose classroom it was. Thanks also to Rod Jones for his careful work on producing the initial transcripts of data from this project, some of which are used in chapter 6, and to all those people who have at some stage read, commented on and made useful suggestions about the material in this book. Any shortcomings remain, of course, wholly my own.

KEY TO TRANSCRIPTION
CONVENTIONS

———— ◆ ————

The transcription conventions I use are adapted from the sequential, turn-by-turn approach to notation for transcribing talk developed by Sacks, Schegloff and (particularly) Jefferson (1974). It is my view, like that of many other researchers into language use, that the process of transcription raises complex and sometimes insurmountable problems for the analyst, and that at best, a data transcript is an incomplete and theoretically-laden artefact (Coates and Thornborrow, 1999). I have tried to capture the detail of relevant interactional features, pauses, overlaps and other aspects of the organisation of the talk, as well as some of the other paralinguistic features in the data that I have considered to be significant, such as volume, pitch variation and marked stress. I am aware of two main problems: firstly, that the symbols can only provide a very basic representation of intonation and prosody; secondly, that the intricacies and detail of multi-party floor interaction are very difficult to capture whatever transcription system is chosen. Particularly in the classroom context, the stave system preferred by some analysts for transcribing this type of data did not seem able to handle the number of participants coming in and out of the talk at any one time, nor the occasional development of parallel floors. Names in the transcripts have been changed where necessary.

Symbols

[---]	previous or subsequent omitted talk at the beginning or end of a turn
(.)	short pause of less than (.5) of a second
(1.3)	timed pause in seconds
hello=	
=hello	latching (no hearable gap) between the end of one turn to the beginning of the next
[good evening]	
[hello]	overlapping talk. [marks the onset of overlap,] marks the end of the overlapping sequence.
(bar)	transcriber's best hearing of indistinct talk
(xxx)	indecipherable talk
((laughs))	para-linguistic features
so in our way	marked stress
OH NO	increased volume
>quick<	marked faster speech delivery
°quietly°	quiet speech delivery
.hh	marked intake of breath
hh.	marked outbreath

Key to transcription conventions

.	falling tone
?	rising tone
,	level tone
ar-	cut off syllable or word
↑oh↓	marked pitch movement

N.B.

The symbols listed above are the conventions I have used in transcribing my own data. Transcripts quoted from other sources may vary in conventions of notation.

POWER, TALK AND INSTITUTIONAL DISCOURSE: SOME KEY CONCEPTS

This book is about talk that takes place in institutional settings. Through some detailed analyses of various contexts for institutional talk, I explore the idea that power relations between the participants in such settings can be observed and analysed as interactional phenomena; that power relations emerge in the interplay between participants' locally constructed, discursive identities and their institutional status. I will therefore be focusing particularly on the practices of talk as interaction, and on the kind of discursive resources that speakers use to get things done in their talk. I also show how speakers are able to draw on those discursive resources in different ways, and with differing outcomes, as the talk unfolds, by examining the relationship between institutional status and the interactional positions this makes available to participants in the talk event.

In this introductory chapter I set out some of the key background concepts that underpin the theoretical and analytic approach I take throughout the book. These are broadly grouped under three main thematic headings: (1) the problem of what we mean by 'institutional' discourse, (2) the relationship between power and language and (3) the available methods we have for analysing this relationship. There will of course be overlaps between these three areas. The concepts of power and social institutions, and the theoretical positions that researchers in the fields of sociolinguistics and discourse analysis adopt in order to analyse them, tend to be intricately linked, so in this introductory chapter I will also try to point out where these links occur and where they are at their strongest.

INSTITUTIONAL DISCOURSE

I begin with the question of institutional discourse — what it is, how it has been characterised and what the problems are in using this as a defining label for certain types of talk. There is now a growing body of research which focuses on talk in institutional settings, from the workplace to the TV studio, but there are still disagreements as to what institutional discourse actually is and how it might be defined. I therefore spend some time in this section discussing the various theoretical positions that characterise current approaches to analysing institutional talk and suggest a working definition for the data analyses I offer in subsequent chapters.

In what ways has 'institutional' discourse been identified as a category of talk which in some way is different from what we might experience as non-institutional or 'conversational' interaction? Jurgen Habermas (1984) described institutional talk as an example of 'strategic discourse', which he distinguished from another form of talk, 'communicative discourse'. Strategic discourse is, he claims, power laden and goal-directed, while communicative discourse, in its ideal manifestation, is about speakers symmetrically engaging in achieving mutual understanding. Harris (1995) points out that Habermas's 'ideal' speech situation remains a theoretical preconstruct, and that in reality, 'communicative action . . . is distorted by power and inequality' (p. 121), and so his description of institutional discourse as a somehow less desirable form of interaction than an idealised form of communication is not particularly helpful if we are dealing with the analysis of empirical data. However, it is nevertheless worth noting that Habermas made a distinction between goal-directed talk, on the one hand, and the achievement of symmetrical understanding, on the other, since these two concepts have played an important role in the way institutional interaction has been characterised in other traditions of research into language in use.

A great deal of the work on talk in institutional settings has been undertaken within the field of conversation analysis (CA). CA traditionally holds that 'ordinary conversation is the predominant medium of interaction in the social world' and that institutional interaction involves 'systematic variation and restriction of activities and their design relative to ordinary conversation' (Drew and Heritage, 1992: 19). These variations and restrictions include speakers' orientation to particular tasks or goals (for example, calls to an emergency service or the delivery of a medical diagnosis), as well as specialised constraints on what 'one or both of the participants will treat as allowable contributions to the business at hand' (p. 22). There are also specialised inferential frameworks for a given institutional context, so how questions are received and interpreted in a job interview, in a news interview or courtroom interaction is very much tied to that specific setting. Steven Levinson (1992) has suggested that the talk that takes place in institutional settings differs from 'non-institutional' conversation in these three essential respects: firstly, it is goal or task oriented; secondly, it involves constraints on what counts as legitimate contributions to that goal or task; and, thirdly, it produces particular kinds of inferences in the way speakers interpret, or orient to, utterances. Describing these constraints on talk, and the specialised, goal-oriented nature of institutional interaction, has been one of the central concerns of conversation analytic approaches to institutional discourse, and there is now a well-established set of findings relating to the organisation of talk in a range of different settings (cf. Drew and Heritage, 1992; Boden, 1994).

Another key concept which is central to the notion of restriction and constraint on talk in interaction is that of 'asymmetry' in talk. In CA this term is most often used to describe the distribution of different types of turns between different participants. Institutional talk has been described as 'characteristically asymmetrical' (Drew and Heritage, 1992: 47) in contrast to ordinary conversational interaction between participants of equal status. For example, in a diagnostic medical interview, the doctor usually asks questions, the patient usually gives answers; similarly, in a courtroom setting, the examining magistrate or attorney asks the questions, the witness gives answers. So what participants do in an institutional setting is to some extent open to description in terms of the types of turns they take.

A rather different view of asymmetry is captured in Habermas's definition of institutional discourse as 'strategic'. For Habermas, asymmetry is much less a question of turn distribution between participants and much more one of unequal distribution of social power and status. But there are also some points of comparison between Habermas's account of institutional discourse and the conventional approach taken by practitioners of conversation analysis. Evident in both is the comparative notion that institutional talk is in some respects different to ordinary conversational talk, as is the reference to goal-oriented aspects of institutional talk. I will return to the question of asymmetry in more detail in chapter 2, but there is an important counterview to this binary division between institutional and ordinary conversational talk that needs to be mentioned here.

In a recent critique of the comparison between ordinary and institutional talk that I have just outlined, Bonnie McElhinny (1997) argues that this comparative account constructs yet another 'false dichotomy' between the two forms of talk (p. 111). She points out that such contrasts between the political and the personal, the economic and the domestic, work and home environments continue to reinforce the distinction between public and private domains of language use, and it is the view of many feminist scholars that this is an ideological distinction which has obscured the political nature of what counts as 'ordinary'. Any analytic approach which regards 'ordinary' conversational talk to be the unmarked, baseline form of social interaction may mask, on the one hand, hierarchies and inequalities that exist in gender, class, ethnic and other social relationships between the participants in 'ordinary' talk and, on the other, the incursion of 'ordinary' talk into contexts for institutional interaction. Consequently, McElhinny suggests that institutional talk is better regarded as a cultural classification, an ideological label which will mean different things to different people.

Where, then, does this leave the analysis of the relationship between social relationships of power and the organisation of talk in such contexts as a school classroom or a radio recording studio? In this book, I describe the contextual settings for my data, using the conventional label of 'institutional'. It will become clear, through the analyses in subsequent chapters, that in these various contexts for talk there is an orientation towards a specific task – the business of the talk as it unfolds is to ask questions, to provide answers (or to resist providing them), to have a discussion, to make a complaint, amongst others. However, these are all activity types that can and surely do just as easily take place outside an identifiable organisational or institutional context. And, similarly, talk that is conventionally associated with non-institutional settings can equally easily occur within settings that are conventionally defined as institutional.[1] In many ways, then, the concept of 'ordinary' talk turns out to be just as problematic, and perhaps just as theoretically pre-constructed, as Habermas's concept of an ideal state of 'communicative discourse'. But, if we think of talk as action, then actions have outcomes, and are taken to accomplish communicative goals in particular social settings. So, rather than defining institutional interaction simply in terms of its points of difference to ordinary talk, I prefer to see it as talk which exhibits a combination of characteristics. This position is still far from satisfactory, and the list of characteristics may well be incomplete, but it attempts to take into account some of the problems inherent in pinning down types of talk as institutional or otherwise. The distinctive features of different kinds of talk in each context will emerge more sharply through the analyses I offer, but some of the primary characteristics are listed below. Institutional talk is, then:

1. Talk that has differentiated, pre-inscribed and conventional participant roles, or identities, whether it takes place in a school classroom, in a TV or radio studio or in a police interview room. In my data these conventional institutional identities include categories such as phone-in host, caller, interviewer, school pupil, policeman.
2. Talk in which there is a structurally asymmetrical distribution of turn types between the participants such that speakers with different institutional identities typically occupy different discursive identities; that is, they get different types of turns in which they do different kinds of things (for example, interviewers conventionally ask questions, interviewees answer them; teachers nominate which pupil will talk next, pupils respond).
3. Talk in which there is also an asymmetrical relationship between participants in terms of speaker rights and obligations. This means that certain types of utterances are seen as legitimate for some speakers but not for others (for example, an examining magistrate is expected to ask questions, a defendant is not).
4. Talk in which the discursive resources and identities available to participants to accomplish specific actions are either weakened or strengthened in relation to their current institutional identities.

In short, institutional discourse can be described as talk which sets up positions for people to talk from and restricts some speakers' access to certain kinds of discursive actions. For instance, in media settings, the role of a TV or radio news interviewer typically (although not exclusively) involves doing the questions, while the role of interviewee involves doing the answers; in the context of a family meal-time, research has shown that children typically are the ones who are asked to tell the story of their day, while it is mostly mothers who elicit the stories and fathers who are the primary recipients, and evaluators, of the events being recounted (Ochs and Taylor, 1992; Blum Kulka, 1997). So, despite being a very different kind of talk event, a family dinner can in many respects be considered to be just as much of an institutional context for talk as a news interview.

I want to close this discussion of what constitutes institutional discourse with two observations made by David Silverman (1997). The first is that '[institutions] structure, but do not determine, what may be said in social settings, how it may be said, and who may say it' (p. 188) and the second is that participants' social roles 'better position some interactants to strategically use available resources to achieve their practical interactional ends, while restricting others' strategic moves' (p. 189). With this in mind, institutional discourse can perhaps be best described as a form of inter-action in which the relationship between a participant's current institutional role (that is, interviewer, caller to a phone-in programme or school teacher) and their current discursive role (for example, questioner, answerer or opinion giver) emerges as a local phenomenon which shapes the organisation and trajectory of the talk. In other words, what people do in institutional encounters is produced, overall, as a result of this interplay between their interactional and discursive role and their insti-tutional identity and status.

POWER

The term 'power' is another conceptual can of worms for discourse analysts; what it is, where it is located and how it can be analysed in or as 'discourse' are all questions that continue to be hotly debated in the broad field of language and discourse studies. Chapter 2 contains a much more detailed discussion of these issues, so here I will only give a preliminary sketch of the concepts of power which have informed sociolinguistic and critical discourse analytic research. The simplest place to start in a discussion of such a complex and highly theorised phenomenon as power is prob-ably with a commonsense, non-theoretical definition. Power means different things to different people; it is multi-faceted, and can take many different forms. It is often seen as a quantifiable thing – some people have more of it than others. Thus we tend to talk about power as measurable in terms of the amount of physical power, polit-ical power, military power, disciplinary power, economic power and so on, that people or organisations might possess. This quantifiable notion of power also means that we can describe some person, or government, or army, or other form of organ-isation as more or less powerful in relation to another. So, for example, in a global political context the president of the US is often seen as wielding considerably more power than the president of a much smaller nation; in the social contexts that are the focus of much sociolinguistic research, men have been regarded as having more power than women, professional middle classes more than impoverished under-classes, white communities more than black communities; in a family context, par-ents more than children. In a commonsense way too, power tends to be associated with rank and status, and hierarchies are built around these relative positions of social, professional and political power. We also conceptualise power in a qualitative way when we talk about such things as a 'powerful performance' or a 'powerful argument', when we describe someone as a 'powerful speaker', and when we talk of 'powerful emotions' or relationships.

But leaving these commonsense understandings of power aside, once we begin to theorise the concept there are complex and often conflicting traditions at work in explaining what power means and what it does. In the paragraphs that follow I set out a necessarily brief and selective discussion of some of the most recent of these traditions which have been the most relevant to the analysis of institutional discourse.

Social theories of power

Within the social sciences there have been various attempts to produce theoretical models of what power is and how it can be seen to work, and these models have been based on some rather different conceptualisations of power. From the behavioural perspective of the early 1960s, power was a matter of individual agency, residing in individuals rather than in organisations (Dahl, 1961). According to this model power can be said to exist only in so far as it is empirically observable in the world, measurable according to people's responses to it (much like the notion of power in physics, where the action of one force can be measured in terms of the effect it has on another). In his succinct discussion of theories of power and ideology, Stuart Clegg (1993) gives the following summary of this view of power and its effects: 'Whatever could not be observed could not be said to be. The unobservable was not seen to be a suitable case for treatment as data' (p. 19).[2]

In contrast to this position is the structural model of power developed by Stephen Lukes (1974), in which power is conceptualised in a much more abstract way, as ideological and hegemonic. Stuart Hall has described the effect of hegemonic power as shaping people's perceptions, cognitions and preferences 'in such a way that [social agents] accept their role in the existing order of things, either because they can see or imagine no alternative to it, or because they see it as natural and unchangeable, or because they see it as divinely ordained or beneficial' (1982: 65). This view of power as an ideological phenomenon and the notion that people accept the prevailing order of things, the world as it is, as natural and unchangeable even though it may not be in their best interests, have been pervasive in many accounts of the relationship between power, ideology and social discourses. They are also to be found in the work of Louis Althusser (1971), who was among the earliest theorists to describe power as a discursive phenomenon. Althusser's account of 'interpellation', and his claim that power operates through discourse by constructing particular subject positions for people to occupy, have been influential in much of the early work in critical discourse analysis (CDA) (cf. Macdonell, 1986).[3] However, more recently it has begun to be superseded by poststructuralist theories which consider identities and subjectivities to be multiple and shifting rather than fixed within a particular ideological structuring, or hegemonic, view of the world.

Pierre Bourdieu's (1992) account of power as 'symbolic capital', whereby some social practices take on more value and status than others, and where knowledge of and access to those practices put some people in potentially more powerful positions than others, has also been found by many sociolinguists to be a productive framework for understanding the relationship between language and power. The notion of 'communities of practice', where language has a symbolic function alongside other symbolic communicative systems (such as dress codes, body language, proxemic behaviours, etc.), has been seen as a more productive alternative to more traditional definitions of a community as a place or population. For Penelope Eckert and Sally McConnell-Ginet (1992), a community of practice is where 'social meaning, social identity, community membership, forms of participation, the full range of community practices, and the symbolic relationship of linguistic form are being constantly and mutually constructed' (p. 492). In this sense every community, from a nuclear family to a company boardroom or a court of law, has a culture of locally constructed values and relations of power; in other words, it forms a community made up of *practices*.

To extend this conceptualisation of power as practice, as a productive process rather than simply a repressive phenomenon, and thus observable in its manifestations at every level of social activity, Michel Foucault (1977, 1980) has provided a guiding theoretical light behind a range of work in the poststructuralist tradition in many areas of sociology, social psychology and particularly in discourse analysis. Foucault resists theorising power it in terms of dominance and ideology, and moves towards a concept of power as a complex and continuously evolving web of social and discursive relations; it is a 'productive network which runs through the whole social body' (1980: 119). This conceptualisation of power has had two important consequences for exploring the relationship between discourse and social, institutional organisations. The first relates to representations of the world through language, and the idea that each society has 'types of discourse which it accepts and makes function as true' (1980: 131). By linking this to the notion of communities of practice, we can begin to see how the social values and 'symbolic capital' that Bourdieu refers to might be discursively constructed in such a community through its conventional linguistic practices; in other words, the prevailing discourses through which it represents, and in some sense constructs, the world. The second consequence relates to interactional practices of language use. Foucault has claimed that 'there are no relations of power without resistances' and that '[these] are formed right at the point where power is exercised' (1980: 142). So, if we want to consider how some forms of language use might be 'powerful', we can look at how this power is instantiated in talk, how it gets activated and how it may be resisted. In other words, what discursive resources do speakers use for 'doing power' in talk, and what resources do others use in response? In the next few paragraphs, I outline some of the analytic possibilities that have emerged from Foucault's highly theorised account of power in discourse.

Discursive power: language as (inter)action

So how can language be powerful? As I have just described, within social theories of power, language, or perhaps more appropriately discourse, has been seen as an important site for both constructing and maintaining power relations. Critical discourse analysts tend to see power as already accruing to some participants and not to others, and this power is determined by their institutional role and their socio-economic status, gender or ethnic identity (Fairclough, 1992; van Dijk, 1993). In this sense, then, social relations of power pre-exist the talk itself; to use Foucault's term, power is already there as 'a regime of truth' (1980: 131). As a result, in CDA, approaching the role of power in discourse tends to be a question of examining how those members of society who possess it, reflect, reinforce and reproduce it through the language they use, in other words, their discourse practices.

The activity of talk itself can be a powerful phenomenon. There are some ways of talking, and some particular types of discursive actions, that have been considered to be more powerful than others. The view that there are more or less powerful ways of speaking underlies much of the early work in sociolinguistic studies of language and gender, which sought to identify differences between the way men and women talk. Robin Lakoff's (1975) list of features which she considered to be typical of women's speech (for example, hedges, use of extreme polite forms, tag questions and 'empty' adjectives) was often taken as the starting point for this avenue of research, although subsequent empirical studies have shown that it is not the linguistic form as such that is powerful or otherwise, rather it is much more a question of who uses it and to what purpose that matters. In other words, it is the use of language in context that will determine the function and the effects of an utterance, and relations of power between speakers may well be central to that contextualised function (O'Barr and Atkins, 1980; Cameron, McAlinden and O'Leary, 1989; Holmes, 1995). As these linguists and others have pointed out, an approach which considers linguistic forms per se as indicators of power (or the lack of it) becomes problematic when one starts to consider the function of silence in interaction (Gal, 1992), or the use of tag questions to threaten or to accuse as well as to mitigate the force of an utterance (Cameron, McAlinden and O'Leary, 1989). There has also sometimes been a tendency to view certain interactional phenomena as discursively powerful. This view contributes to what I call the 'territorial' concept of power in language (see chapter 2), where levels of discursive power are analysed in terms of access to, and successful occupation of, the conversational 'floor' (Edelsky, 1981). Don Zimmerman and Candace West's (1975) study of patterns of interruption between women and men, where the amount of interruption was taken as an indicator of asymmetrical power relations between speakers, is one example of this tendency.

However, rather than considering discursive power to be a property of particular types of utterances, or the amount of space within which someone can get to talk, the approach I adopt to power in this book is to see it as a contextually sensitive phenomenon, as a set of resources and actions which are available to speakers and which can be used more or less successfully depending on who the speakers are and what kind of speech situation they are in. From this perspective, power is accomplished in discourse both on a structural level, through the turn and type of space speakers are given or can get access to, and, on an interactional level, through what they can effectively accomplish in that space. In other words, I am suggesting that linguistic forms are available to speakers as discursive resources that can be drawn upon to accomplish actions in talk; however, the function and effects of these resources are always an outcome of the interactional context in which they occur. This context is partly constructed by the local, situated talk and the shifting interplay of interactional relations between speakers, and partly defined by the institutional relationships that hold between them.

Discursive power: language as representation

Although my primary analytic focus in this book is on talk and interaction, the representational aspects of discursive power also need to be mentioned here. Susan Gal (1992) has suggested that 'the strongest form of power may well be the ability to define social reality, to impose visions of the world. Such visions are inscribed in language and, most importantly, enacted in interaction' (p. 160). In order to analyse how discourse can be powerful, we need to take into account not just how speakers get to say what they do, but what it is that they say. In other words, what kind of role does power play in the negotiation and construction of meaning? There are some environments for talk where participants share common, consensual representations of the world, and other environments where those representations are conflicting. For example, in a study of American small claims court disputes, it was found that those litigants who used 'rule-oriented' accounts in presenting their case fared better than those who used 'relational' accounts. Rule-oriented accounts, in which litigants presented a theory of events, with the attendant rules and violations, were seen as more congruent with the 'logic' of the law courts than relational accounts, which typically contained details of the complex relationships or series of events involved in a case. These were often construed as inappropriate and irrelevant by the courts (Conley and O'Barr, 1990). So representational accounts of the way things are in the world can also be more or less appropriate, more or less powerful, depending on the context in which they are produced (again, I will take up this point in more detail in chapter 2). An important theme in the book is therefore this reflexive relationship between talk and its institutional context: social meanings are jointly produced by participants in talk, but talk is always grounded within a specific, local context.

Finally, I want to stress that power is not, of course, only an issue in talk that occurs in institutional settings, but it is often the case that institutional settings are more easily accessible as a source of data for analysts than other settings of more 'ordinary' talk. It is questionable whether there can ever be such a thing as totally symmetrical talk, or talk that is not ultimately goal oriented in some way,[4] and, as I have pointed out, although conversation has often been used as a baseline for what is taken to be symmetrical talk between participants of equal status, it is not clear to me that this position is necessarily a justifiable one. If power is a phenomenon which is observable at every level of social interaction, as Foucault has claimed, then it must also be observable in the interplay between participants in all forms of, and occasions for, talk. From the analytic perspective I adopt in this book, the difference between ordinary conversation and institutionally shaped interaction is that in institutional talk the identity of speakers, their institutional roles and relationships are already established by the context. In conversational interaction, where the social roles of participants may not be so clearly contextually structured or institutionally defined, it becomes more difficult to make any analytical assumptions about what counts as a powerful discursive action and what does not. That is not to say that such actions are not taking place, but only that they may not be recoverable from the talk and available for analysis in the same way.

METHODS

Under this third thematic heading I deal with the question of methodology and the reasons I have chosen to work with an analytic framework which draws on three distinct traditions of research in language and interaction. The approach I take to data is primarily a qualitative one, and owes much to the findings of CA and CDA as well as to the socio-interactional work of Erving Goffman. While none of these separate fields requires any real introduction here, in this section I explain why I have found that combining the insights from these different theoretical approaches to talk provides an appropriate set of questions and analytic tools to account for the ways in which power emerges as a discursive phenomenon in the context of institutional interaction.

Many of the existing studies of power in discourse have been predicated on the assumption that the social and institutional roles of the participants (for example, doctor/patient, teacher/pupil, magistrate/defendant) construct similarly asymmetrical relationships between them of dominance and subordination, with speakers occupying respectively a more powerful or a less powerful position. Much less attention has been given to how these issues of power are constantly under negotiation by participants in the talk. The question of how speakers manage their compliance with, and/or their resistance to, the discursive practices through which those relationships are constructed on a local, interactional level is a fundamental one in this book. To engage with this question, I have collected my conceptual and analytic tools from three main sources.

In order to conceive of power as an analysable phenomenon in discourse in the first place, I acknowledge my debt to the field of CDA and particularly my early encounters with some of the seminal work in this area (Kress and Hodge, 1979; Chilton, 1985; van Dijk, 1985; Fairclough, 1989). From CDA then, I take the central premise that language is a social phenomenon, and that language in use is inextricably bound up with other social phenomena (I describe this work more fully, and the contribution made to the debates about power and language by critical discourse analysts, in chapter 2).

The approach to power that I will adopt for the analysis of institutional talk in this book is based on Foucault's conceptualisation of the relationship between power and discourse, as I have outlined in section 2 above.[5] Essentially, this means that power is observable in interaction through the shifting web of discursive positions and actions that speakers take up in talk and through the range of discursive resources available to them. The key questions then become: what kind of access is available to these resources, and to which participants, and with what kind of consequences? In order to answer these questions, I have drawn primarily on the analytical tools of CA. Taking the view that language in interaction is fundamental to the production of social phenomena, that it is through language as social action that participants structure, organise, order and make sense of their experience of the world, CA holds that talk is always both context shaping and context shaped (Heritage, 1984). In other words, utterances become meaningful and are understood through their sequential placement in their local environment, that is, the continually developing sequence of talk in which they occur. A speaker's utterance, occurring as a turn at talk, is analysable and accountable in relation to the situated context of another, prior utterance, and, in turn, sets up the context for a next utterance. But talk is also sensitive to its wider environment, and this can be seen in the way participants design and make sense of utterances in relation to the current context of interaction. For example, broadcast talk is designed not just for its immediate recipients, but, crucially, also for the audience, and this can be shown by attending to the sequential and interactional features of talk in these settings (Drew and Heritage, 1992). I will return to a more extensive discussion of relevant work in CA later in the book, for the moment it will suffice to say that, in its attention to the fine detail of talk, the methods it offers are some of the most productive in the analysis of institutional data, despite its well-documented caution (see, for example, Schegloff, 1997) in directly addressing broader theoretical issues associated with the discursive analysis of social and institutional power relations.

Finally, the insights of Erving Goffman (1981, 1983), on social interaction and the 'interaction order', have consistently, if not always explicitly, informed my thinking about how language provides us the rich resources with which to do so much of our interactional work. In particular, the concepts of facework, footing and participation frameworks in social occasions for talk have proved to be some of the most useful analytic constructs in describing the contextual and participatory features of the data I analyse here.

THE STRUCTURE OF THE BOOK

The rest of the book comprises a critical discussion of a range of perspectives that have been taken in analysing the relationship between power and language, followed by a series of case studies that focus on specific aspects of talk in institutional contexts. In chapter 2, I trace the origins and development of CDA and give an overview of some of the key work, in this and other areas of sociolinguistic research, which has made an important contribution to our understanding of language, power and institutional discourse. Chapters 3, 4, 5 and 6 all contain analyses of different interactional features, using data from four main institutional settings. These include radio phone-ins, television and radio interviews, a police interview and a primary school classroom. In each case, I describe how the structural design of the talk, as institutional interaction, provides particular types of turn positions for participants, which set up corresponding discursive identities for them to talk from. Through these analyses, I explore how speakers' discursive roles intermesh with their institutional roles and identify the kind of discursive resources that they are able to draw upon by looking in detail at the interactional organisation of the talk.

To conclude this introduction, a brief word about the data. Chapter 3 is based on a discussion of a police interview with a woman making a complaint of rape. This was broadcast in a series of documentary programmes about a British police force in the early 1980s. The data in chapter 4 are taken from a BBC Radio One phone-in programme during the general election of 1987. Chapter 5 is an analysis of interview talk recorded from TV and radio sources from 1987 onwards, and chapter 6 is based on data recorded in a primary school classroom in London during 1998/99. Unless otherwise stated, all the transcripts are my own. A key to the system of transcription and symbols is given on page (ix).

NOTES

1. Maynard however points out that rather than being a 'unique species of interaction', institutional talk is 'in many ways continuous with ordinary life' (1992: 355).
2. Echos of this view can be found in the notion of contextual relevance in conversation analysis, which I address more fully in chapter 2.
3. This has been particularly the case in discourse analysis which has been influenced by Marxist philosophy and traditions of thought.
4. As an example, Jen Coates (1996) found that the talk of women friends may be in one sense symmetrical, but is nevertheless perceived as fulfilling the important goal of accomplishing friendship by the participants. The talk then has a social goal in this context, rather than a task-based goal of getting a medical diagnosis done, getting a politician to answer a question or a class of children to have a discussion.
5. One of the clearest accounts of Foucault's work and its relevance to discourse analysis can be found in Norman Fairclough's discussion of language and social change (Fairclough, 1992).

2

◆

PERSPECTIVES ON POWER: APPROACHES TO THE CRITICAL ANALYSIS OF LANGUAGE AND INTERACTION

Since most work which addresses the question of power in discourse does so from its own particular analytical perspective, it is unusual to find an account of the various different approaches to analysing language, power and interaction which deals with the wide spectrum of theoretical positions that have emerged within the fields of sociolinguistics and discourse analysis, broadly defined. In this chapter I attempt to go some way towards providing that account by outlining some of the major work which has contributed to the analysis of language and power, and by presenting a critical view of ways that power has been conceptualised, theorised and analysed in that work. I begin with an overview of the early studies in CDA, followed by a discussion of some key current theoretical perspectives, then move on to show how the issue of power has been dealt with in practice across a range of empirical research in discourse and conversation analysis.

Over the past few decades there has been a growing interest in the analysis of language as a form of social, institutional and symbolic power, moving language study out of the domain of 'langue',[1] where linguistic forms are decontextualised and treated as a cognitive, mental phenomenon, into to the domain of 'parole', where language is regarded as a socially situated, discursive and therefore often an ideological phenomenon. Many of the studies in the latter domain have drawn productively on the writings of social theorists, principally Foucault (1972, 1977, 1980), Bourdieu (1992) and Habermas (1982); the work of Althusser (1971), Bakhtin (1981, 1986) and Pecheux (1982) has also had its part to play in the development of current thinking on the relationship between power and language. Ironically enough, although much of these theorists' work was directly concerned with the social significance of language, their observations generally remained on the level of abstraction and there was very little in the way of empirical data upon which they based their conceptual claims. One of the aims of research in discourse analysis has been to examine real instances of naturally occurring texts and talk in the light of these theoretical concepts about the relationship between language, society and power.[2]

This move from hypothetical examples to real language data has exposed a set of complex questions about what kind of claims the analysis of discourse can (and cannot) make about social relations of power. In the following pages, I explore some of the issues raised by these questions and outline what I believe to be the most significant and productive aspects of the debate. This discussion therefore also provides an important backdrop to the approach I take to analysing the data presented in subsequent chapters of the book.

CRITICAL LINGUISTICS

Early studies in the field of critical linguistics, generally taken to be the precursor of the broader field of critical discourse analysis as it has developed over the past two decades, were based on the premise that grammar is an ideological instrument for the categorisation and classification of things that happen in the world (Fowler *et al.*, 1979; Kress and Hodge, 1979; Hodge and Kress, 1993). This premise owed much to the theory of linguistic determinism known as the 'Sapir/Whorf hypothesis' (cf. Crystal, 1987), which holds two fundamental assumptions: (1) that the language we use (through its classificatory and representational systems) influences the way we think and (2) that languages are different, that is, no two linguistic systems have the same way of categorising the world. What has now become known as the 'weak version' of this hypothesis, that we see and hear things as we do, perceive and categorise our experience in certain ways because of the language habits of our community which predispose us to making certain interpretive choices, is still central to many accounts of the relationship between language, power and ideologies, and particularly to those accounts which analyse discourse as a representational (rather than an interactional) practice.

The critical linguists set out to analyse language as 'text' or 'discourse', rather than as decontextualised sets of possible sentences in the Chomskyan tradition. Basing their analytical approach mainly on Halliday's (1978, 1985) systemic/functional grammar, and his model of representational, interpersonal and textual levels of language, their aim was to demystify the discourse of commonsense ideologies by showing that the grammatical and semantic forms which create a text are only selections from a range of possible linguistic forms; that as a result, 'all perception involves theory or ideology and there are no "raw" uninterpreted, theory-free facts' (Trew, 1979: 95). So it then becomes possible to compare two (or more) accounts of the same event in terms of their grammatical and representational structure, as for instance in Tony Trew's (1979) analysis of reports of the violence at the 1977 Notting Hill Carnival in London, or Martin Montgomery's (1986a) account of the press coverage of the 1985 miners' strike in Britain.

The critical linguists' development of a theory of language as a form of social practice, where 'the rules and norms that govern linguistic behaviour have a social function, origin and meaning' (Hodge and Kress, 1993: 204), represented a significant step in the move towards a critical analysis of language use, where the links between social relations of power and particular instances of discursive practice could be explored. However, this theory has been applied mainly to texts which are essentially 'planned' discourses (Ochs, 1979), such as newspaper reports, television news reports, political speeches, and the like, rather than spontaneous, naturally occurring spoken interaction. Furthermore, their analyses tended to be based on the idea that power and ideology are visible in systems of pre-determined and socially fixed meanings, rather than on a concept of power in discourse as something plural, negotiable and constantly shifting.

One of the main problems with the critical linguistic approach to power was its limiting focus on grammatical and lexical choice. Selections in grammatical form, and established patterns of representation, tend to be more a product of the situated social and cultural environments in which they occur than of the limitations of a grammatical system, and, as Trevor Pateman (1980) has pointed out, grammar cannot be considered to be 'at fault' in giving rise to selective representations. It is rather a question of whose meanings prevail and in which contexts that matters.[3]

Although the critical linguists ran into difficulties in terms of the conceptual underpinning of their theory (mapping world view on to linguistic structure has been criticised as reductive, as well as analytically insensitive to the range of possible meanings that a text can display to different groups of readers), their contribution to establishing the field of critical discourse analysis was substantial, and subsequent research (for example, Montgomery, 1986a; Fairclough, 1989; Fowler, 1991; Mills, 1995; Simpson, 1993) has drawn productively on the concept of variation and selection in grammatical and representational form to explain how language can work to produce contrasting versions of reality from different ideological perspectives.

DEVELOPING THE THEORY: CRITICAL DISCOURSE ANALYSIS

Perhaps the most comprehensive and programmatic attempt to develop a theory which links discourse, power and social structure can be found in the work of Norman Fairclough (1989, 1992, 1995). Fairclough's main concern has been to examine the role of social institutions in shaping discourse practices, and his theoretical position is that all forms of discourse are determined by sets of institutional conventions which are in turn shaped by wider social relations of power (1989: 17). From the courtroom to the family dinner table, from a problem page letter to a university prospectus, Fairclough argues that the language we use is always shaped by the material and social conditions in which it is produced, and that 'in so producing their world [as "orderly" or "accountable"] members' practices are shaped in ways of which they are usually unaware by social structures, relations of power, and the nature of the social practice they are engaged in whose stakes always go beyond producing meanings' (1992: 72).

Fairclough describes discourse as a 'three-dimensional' concept involving texts (the objects of linguistic analysis), discourse practices (the production, distribution and consumption of texts) and social practices (the power relations, ideologies and hegemonic struggles that discourses either reproduce, challenge or in some way restructure). As a consequence of this three-dimensional model, Fairclough argues that the first dimension, the text, cannot be effectively analysed without taking into account the other two dimensions. His aim is therefore to build up a framework for analysing texts (a term which he uses to apply to both written and spoken instances of language use), which will enable them to be treated as instances of discursive and social practices.[4] According to this framework, different levels of linguistic structure (for example, lexis, transitivity choices, semantic collocation, metaphoric relations, etc.) can be used to build up a critical account of both the relational and the representational aspects of discourse, corresponding to Halliday's interpersonal and ideational functions of language.

Discourse is thus, on the one hand, the construction of interpersonal social relations through features such as interactional control, turn-taking, exchange structure, topic control, agenda setting, formulating, modality and politeness; on the other, it constructs social reality through textual features such as argument structure and cohesion, transitivity and theme, wording and lexical choice and metaphorical meanings in texts. All these textual elements have then to be interpreted and shown to be significant in some way in relation not just to their context, or the immediate situation, but also to the broader social structures within which they are produced. For Fairclough, then, discourse is textual, material and social; meanings are always shaped, produced and otherwise determined according to and within prevailing ideological frameworks and social power relations.

How does this approach to discourse work in practice? Since my purpose in this book is to focus on institutional spoken interaction, I turn as a first example to one of Fairclough's analyses of institutional spoken discourse: a transcript of a medical interview taken from Mishler (1984) where a patient is being examined for a stomach complaint. I have reproduced sections of the transcript of the medical interview as it appears in Fairclough (1992: 138–9). The doctor (D) is male, the patient (P) is female.

Extract (1)

```
 1. D: Hm hm ... Now what do you mean by a sour stomach?
 2. P: ... What's a sour stomach? A heartburn
 3.    like a heartburn or someth[ing.
 4. D:                           [Does it burn over here?
 5. P:                                                    Yea:h.
 6.    It li- I think- I think it like- If you take a needle
 7.    and stick [ya right [... there's a pain right here [...
 8. D:           [Hm hm    [Hm hm                          [Hm hm
 9. P: and and then it goes from here on this side to this side.
10. D: Hm hm Does it [go into the back?
11. P:              [It's a:ll up here. No. It's all right
12.    [up here in front
13. D: [Yeah           And when do you get that?
14.                                              ...
```

```
15. P: ... Wel:l when I eat something wrong.
16. D:                             How- How
17.    soon after you eat it?
18. P:                  ... Wel:l
19.    ... probably an hour ... maybe [less
20. D:                               [about an hour?
21. P: Maybe less ... I've cheated and I've been
22.    drinking which I shouldn't have done.
```

What can be made of these data? In his analysis of this example, which he describes as typical of 'standard' medical practice, Fairclough argues that the doctor is in control of the interactional organisation of the interview on several levels. Firstly, he controls the way turns are distributed in the talk, by initiating a cycle of questions that the patient has to answer, and then assessing her response to them before moving on to the next question in the cycle. So essentially the doctor does the questions, while the patient does the answers. The doctor also asks 'closed' questions which constrain the kind of answers the patient can provide. His questions (for example, lines 1, 4, 10, 13, 16 of the transcript) are all designed to elicit specific information about the patient's condition (when do you get that? how soon? how much?), and he also controls what counts as an adequate answer by accepting the patient's response mainly by continuing his questioning or with a response token like 'yeah' (line 13). Secondly, he controls the topics, pursuing medical detail rather than other problems alluded to by the patient, for instance her drinking (lines 21 and 22). Fairclough finds evidence of this kind of topic in the following section of the transcript (extract (2)), where the doctor pursues precise answers to his questions, 'One or two drinks a day', 'How many drinks –' (line 10) and 'How long is that' (line 19), rather than taking up the problematic issues introduced by the patient of sleep troubles (line 5) and later marriage troubles (line 18).

Extract (2)

```
 1. D: [Does drinking make it worse?
 2. P: [(...)                    Ho ho uh ooh Yes ...
 3.    ... Especially the carbonation and the alcohol.
 4. D: ... Hm hm ... How much do you drink?
 5. P: ... I don't know ... Enough to make me
 6.    go to sleep at night ... and that's quite a bit.
 7. D: One or two drinks a day?
 8. P:                       O:h no no no humph it's
 9.    (more like) ten. [... at night.
10. D:                  [How many drinks- a night.
11. P:                                  At night.
12. D:                                        ...
13.    ... Whaddya ta- what type of drinks? ... I[(...)-
14. P:                                  [Oh vodka
15.    ... yeah vodka and ginger ale.
16. D:                      ...
17.    ... How long have you been drinking that heavily?
18. P: ... Since I've been married.
19. D: ... How long is that?
20. P:                    (giggle ...) Four years. (giggle)
```

He argues that by only taking up some of the topics raised by the patient, the doctor is working through a pre-set agenda in a three-part, 'question, response, assessment' cycle, resisting the voice of the 'life world' introduced into the talk by the patient, and imposing the voice of the medical world (Mishler, 1984). The patient, on the other hand, has to be more accommodating to the voice of the medical world. Fairclough does however acknowledge that it is possible to take a different approach to these data, by focusing more on the conflictual aspects of the talk, which arise because of the struggle between these two voices, between the 'technological rationality' of the doctor and the 'commonsense rationality' of the patient (p. 144). Seen from this perspective, he concedes that the talk may be 'more fragmented and rather less well ordered than if one views it as a manifestation of doctor control' (p. 143).

I now want to examine more closely this view of what constitutes 'order' in talk. For the talk to proceed 'smoothly at an organisational level' (p. 139), Fairclough suggests that turns have to be evenly distributed, topics established, questions answered, etc. According to this analysis, it is the doctor, the institutional 'voice', who ensures that the interview with the patient proceeds along these lines; in other words, the doctor effectively does the controlling through his institutionally established discursive role as questioner and topic selector, and thus produces orderly talk.

Another way of looking at this example of doctor–patient interaction is to see it as orderly because of the collaborative effort of both participants. An alternative view of order in talk is to conceive of order as something which is accomplished jointly between speakers, rather than imposed by exterior, contextual structures (Sacks, Schegloff and Jefferson, 1974). The activity of taking turns at talk is by its very nature 'orderly', whether that talk is casual conversation, a medical interview or an argument. From this analytic standpoint, the doctor and patient are both engaged in accomplishing the business of a medical interview, and control of the talk is not something that is invested in either one or other of the participants. The talk may be described as 'asymmetrical'[5] in the distribution of different types of turns, in so far as one participant does most of the questions and the other most of the answers, but that asymmetry is not necessarily indicative of a dominant/subordinate social relationship between the speakers. In other words, 'doctor' and 'patient' cannot be taken as inherently powerful, or powerless, roles in and of themselves. I will return to this perspective in more detail later in this chapter, and also in subsequent chapters in relation to interaction across a range of different institutional contexts, but for the moment I want to take another look at the talk represented in this doctor/patient data transcript from a more conversation analytic perspective.

One problem with the type of approach to discourse taken by Fairclough is that it imposes a pre-conceived institutional structure on the data, rather than dealing with it on a turn-by-turn basis. For example, both Fairclough and Mishler analysed this sequence in terms of a series of three-part 'exchanges'[6] with a question/response/acceptance format, where the acceptance slot (which is also referred to as 'assessment' (p. 142)) can be either implicit or explicit. Thus, a follow-up question from the doctor is treated as an implicit acceptance (or assessment) of the patient's previous turn as an answer. This three-part structure is central to the claim that the doctor is 'controlling the basic interaction' by opening and closing each cycle and accepting/acknowledging the patient's responses. The patient's turns at talk are seen as sandwiched in by the surrounding, controlling turns of the doctor. Furthermore, the doctor is described as 'offering' turns to the patient, while 'taking' them himself (p. 140). In practice, the metadiscourse used here, which refers to one speaker controlling, offering and taking turns, imposes an interpretation of the data which may be misleading. While it seems clear that this particular form of institutional practice, the medical interview, operates within constraints of time and efficiency, which affect the kind of talk that takes place in it, it is not so clear that the notion of power can be evoked in these terms. Indeed, Fairclough goes on to compare this form of medical interview with another form, more typical of 'alternative' medical practice, where more time is taken to give patients the space to talk. In these interviews the doctor asks more open questions and the patient takes longer response turns, yet the doctor is still considered to be in control of the talk, albeit less overtly, through asking medically important questions, offering assessments and opening and closing the interview.

To return to the medical interview in extract (1), it is possible to see how the doctor and patient work collaboratively in jointly constructing this talk. In the first question/answer pair, the patient (P) pauses for over one second before reformulating the doctor's (D) question:

```
1. D: Now what do you mean by a sour stomach?
2. P: ... What's a sour stomach?' A heartburn
3.    like a heartburn or someth[ing.
4. D:                           [Does it burn over here?
5. P:                                            Yea:h
```

D then takes up P's description in his next question turn, using her word 'burn'. The overlap between the two turns, when D asks his next question about where the pain is located (lines 3 and 4), is so close to a turn completion point that it does not appear to be a violative, or 'power-oriented', interruption (Goldberg, 1990). P's next turn seems to constitute more than just an answer to D's previous question, as her turn could have been complete after 'Yeah' (line 5). What happens is that she then self selects as 'continuing speaker' hesitantly at first with three false starts (line 6), and goes on to describe the location of the pain. D's next turns are placed as minimal responses to P's description, indicating his role as recipient and his attention to that description. At line 10, there is a substantial stretch of overlapping speech where P starts her turn after D in order to complete her description:

```
10. D: Hm hm Does it [go into the back?
11. P:               [It's all up here. No. It's all right
12.    [up here in front
13. D: [Yeah            And when do you get that?
```

When we look at the actual detail of the way these speakers take their turns in this sequence, it becomes more difficult to describe the interaction straightforwardly as a series of three-part structures initiated and terminated by the doctor, who 'offers' turns to P. P does not just answer D's questions by taking the offered turn, but also self selects as next speaker. In line 11, she starts talking *before* D has completed his turn at line 10 in order to continue her response about the location of the pain. It is only after she has done this that she attends to D's question 'Does it go into the back?' with a direct answer 'No'. In the same turn, she repeats the overlapped part of her utterance in a way that both enables her to reaffirm her preceding description, and to respond to D's question about 'the back' with a contrasting location: 'It's all *right* up here *in the front*' (my emphasis).

From this reading of the data transcript,[7] what goes on here in interactional terms seems to be much more complex than a recurring three-turn sequence. If we count each change of speaker as constituting a new turn, including D's minimal response turns, then there are eight turns in this sequence, starting from D's question in line 4 'Does it burn over here?' as far as his final receipt token 'Yeah' in line 13, when the topic is changed to another aspect of P's condition, the 'when' question. In this sequence, the patient does not just answer the doctor's 'yes/no' question, she produces a description of the pain, which the doctor receives with minimal response turns (first overlapping the patient when she pauses in her description). There is also an overlapping stretch of talk between the two speakers in lines 11 and 12, where the patient finishes one answer before responding to the doctor's next question. So the division of the talk into a basic three-turn cycle misses some of the intricate interactional work going on here. There is another instance of overlap in extract 2 (lines 1 and 2) where P self selects as next speaker at the same time as D:

```
1. D: [Does drinking make it worse?
2. P: [(...)                        Ho ho uh ooh Yes.
```

Here, P's overlapping speech is unclear, but according to the transcript there is a 0.8 second pause immediately preceding this overlap. This leaves the floor momentarily open to either speaker, and indeed both start to speak simultaneously, although P concedes the floor to D's next question. Later on in the transcript there is also a moment when the three-turn model cannot adequately describe the interaction. In the sequence where they are dealing with how much P drinks, the following exchange occurs:

```
 7. D: One or two drinks a day?
 8. P:                    O:h no no no humph it's
 9.    (more like) ten.  [... at night.
10. D:                   [How many drinks- a night.
11. P:                                    At night.
```

The overlapping stretch is interesting here, as D asks his second question, 'How many drinks', *after* P has already given him the answer. Now this could be considered 'disorderly', as questions generally appear before answers, and indeed some repair work follows by D to put this right. He leaves his 'how many' question unfinished, but acknowledges receipt of P's answer by repeating the final part of her utterance, 'a night'. That he chooses to acknowledge the time rather than the quantity is another significant detail in so far as P has explicitly marked the contrast with D's proposed time scale, 'a day', so he in turn marks his orientation to this precision about *when* she drinks. Just as she did in the earlier, pain-locating sequence, here P pursues her answer in spite of the fact that D has started another question, rather than relinquishing the floor to him. Moreover, it is P who finishes this sequence with a confirmation of D's receipt turn, 'at night', so we get the following schematic pattern:

```
D: question 1
P:            > response 1
D:                [question 2 abandoned] > receipt
P:                                       > confirmation of receipt.
```

In working through this data transcript using an analytic approach based on a sequential model of interaction, rather than the three-part exchange structure model proposed by Fairclough, I have tried to show that, when we begin to look at the detail of the talk, it becomes less clear that we can describe the operation of power in discourse in terms of one participant 'controlling' the turn-taking organisation. While it seems clear that this talk constitutes a particular form of institutional discursive practice, that speaker identities and participant status are asymmetrical, and that there is an institutional agenda at work here (the business of symptom description, diagnosis and subsequent proposed treatment), I would question Fairclough's interpretation of the doctor as doing things like 'controlling questions' and the patient as doing things like 'accepting' turns (p. 144). As we saw on two occasions in the talk, P pursued her own turn without waiting for D's offer, and, on one occasion, D abandoned a question entirely in response to the way P had designed her preceding turn.

To summarise, then. From the critical discourse analytic perspective which is exemplified in Fairclough's work, all talk, be it everyday conversation, a doctor's consultation, classroom discussion or a political interview, is viewed as taking place within social structural parameters and according to conventions of social and discursive practices. Most crucially, talk is not simply 'an accomplishment of the social actors who produce it' (1989: 12). Indeed Fairclough is critical of this position, which he ascribes to much of the work in CA, because it tends to naturalise the commonsense view that talk 'just happens', regardless of where, when and with whom. For Fairclough, all interaction is subject to the social and institutional constraints of the context in which it is produced, constraints that lead to the reproduction of existing relations of power and status.

I now want to turn to a contrasting view of talk and social context. In the following section, I explore what a conversation analytic perspective might bring to the analysis of power in discourse.

CONVERSATION ANALYSIS AND THE QUESTION OF 'ASYMMETRY'

Firmly on the other side of the theoretical and methodological fence, CA has traditionally had very little to say about the question of power in social interaction. In fact, most conversation analysts have consistently maintained that contextual features of the talk have to be shown to be oriented to by participants themselves before any claims at all can be made about why people say and do what they do. This position has been justified by Emmanuel Schegloff (1991) as follows:

> If it is to be argued that some legal, organizational or social environment underlies the participants' organizing of some occasion of talk in interaction in some particular way, either one *can* show the details in the talk which that argument allows us to notice, and which in return supply the demonstrable warrant for the claim by showing the relevant presence of the sociological context in the talk; or one *cannot* point to such detail. . . .
> either there is a proximate, conversationally represented indication of the relevance, or the aspects of context which have been invoked, in which case invocations of more remote context are unnecessary, or there is no conversationally represented indication of the relevance of the aspects of context which have been invoked, in which case the warrant for invoking it has not been established. (p. 65)

Schegloff's position is that however strong the analyst's intuitions may be that the social roles people occupy, and the context for the talk, are playing some crucial part in the kind of talk that is going on, this cannot be assumed in any *a priori* way, but must be shown to be the case empirically from the data at hand. As a result, conversation analytic studies of talk in institutional settings tend to use the term 'asymmetries' in discourse (for example, in the context of legal discourse, Atkinson and Drew, 1979; in medical interaction, Ten Have, 1991), rather than assume that there are pre-inscribed, structurally defined participant roles, rights or 'positions' which people typically get to speak from, or that there are specific kinds of things they typically get to say in those positions. The problem is that this aseptic use of the term 'asymmetry' can mask what may be essentially inherent inequalities in speakers' access to, and effective use of, discursive resources.

However, there have been some recent studies which push at these paradigmatic boundaries by attempting to bring issues of power into the analytic frame of CA. Ian Hutchby (1996b) makes a persuasive argument that CA *can* deal with issues of power in his analysis of the argument sequences between host and caller in a talk radio show. Hutchby shows that power can be analysed as a discursive phenomenon by examining the opening structure, or 'design', of calls to the show, which requires the caller to 'go first' and express their point of view on some issue before the host, who 'goes second'. In argumentative discourse, second position is claimed to be more powerful than first position in that it enables the host 'to critique or attack the caller's line simply by exhibiting scepticism about its claims, challenging the agenda relevance of assertions, or taking the argument apart by identifying minor inaccuracies in its details' (1996b: 495).

From a rather different perspective and different institutional context, David Silverman's (1997) study of the discourse and practice of HIV counselling is an attempt to show how forms of discursive power and resistance can be analysed precisely through their local reproduction in talk. Indeed, Silverman explicitly sets out to combine a 'bottom-up' micro-analysis of talk in counselling sessions, based on conversation analytic techniques, with a 'top-down' macro-analysis informed by Foucauldian concepts of power and knowledge, arguing that this blending of perspectives makes it possible to analyse how power relations are both embedded in institutional discourse and constructed within social interactions. Consequently he can begin to address not just the 'how' question central to CA – how do counsellors and their clients conduct and organise their talk in these settings – but also to ask some of the 'why' questions that Schegloff so steadfastly eschews in his methodological approach – what is it about this specific institutional context that may shape the kind of talk that people do in it? Silverman justifies this combined approach by implicitly posing a further question – where does the analysis take us if the 'why' questions are not asked?[8] Through his empirical study of interaction in these contexts, Silverman is able to set out some implications for counselling practice, providing insights into the different counselling formats, and thus developing practitioners' understanding of how to manage these often sensitive and difficult encounters.

While they differ in aim and in analytical focus (Silverman is using the techniques of CA to describe a particular form of discourse practice within the problematic, troubled context of HIV counselling, whereas Hutchby is describing a specific pattern of sequential interaction between host and caller in a talk radio show, within which power can be identified as a structural discursive phenomenon), significant in these two studies is their common appeal to Foucault's (1977, 1980) theoretical concept of power as a constantly shifting set of relations which can be analysed in the detail of localised forms of interaction.

So, in spite of Fairclough's objection that conversation analysts' dismissal of context naturalises the concept that talk just 'happens', and in spite of Schegloff's objection to invoking context as having any relevance whatsoever unless participants display some orientation to it, both the above accounts demonstrate in their different ways that it is in fact possible to begin to approach the discursive construction and negotiation of power through attending closely to the details of talk. What is more, Silverman's study also demonstrates practical outcomes of this approach which can lead to possible recommendations for changes in forms of institutional discursive practice.

Questions of power and social status are never far from the surface in many other studies of language use which have been less concerned with, and constrained by, the kind of theoretical and methodological paradigms I have just outlined here. In between the two somewhat polarised positions of CDA and CA lies a broad spectrum of research which draws on both sociolinguistic theories of variation and pragmatic theories of communication, broadly defined, to account for the role of power in discursive interaction. In the rest of this chapter I move on from the theoretical concerns of CDA and CA, to a discussion of a range of different studies which have addressed the issue of power in some of the key areas of discourse analysis. I begin with some of the research which has focused on the use of questioning as a powerful discursive action.

QUESTIONS AS A POWERFUL RESOURCE

The way that people use questions as a potentially powerful interactive resource has long been recognised by researchers in discourse and conversation analysis. In one of his early lectures, Harvey Sacks (1995) observed how young children use questions like 'you know what?' (which usually get a response of 'what?') as a way of dealing with their restricted rights to talk, and improving their chances of getting past the initial stage of conversations with adults. According to Sacks, there are two basic 'rules' of two-party conversations: firstly, if one person asks a question, the other answers it, and, secondly, the person who asked the question can talk again after the other answers, and can ask another question. Children astutely turn this rule around by making sure that they get a chance to say what they had to say in the first place by setting up the other person as questioner, thereby putting themselves in the position of answerer:

It happens to be that the question they elicit with their question has altogether open form, and what stands as an answer is whatever the kid takes to be an answer, and thereby provides him with the opportunity to say what it is he wanted to say in the first place. However, not on his own say-so, but under obligation.   (Vol. I: 256)

The discursive position of questioner or answerer thus seems to have certain perceived rights and obligations accruing to it, and speakers use these positions to shift their status in relation to other participants in conversational interaction.

The particular nature of the questioning process that takes place in courtroom settings has been the object of extensive research from many different perspectives (for example Harris, 1984; O'Barr and Atkins, 1980; Atkinson and Drew, 1979). Sandra Harris specifically looks at the function of particular types of question formats as a powerful means of discursive control in British magistrates' courts examinations. In her analysis of the questioning procedures in these courts, Harris analysed the range of syntactic forms the magistrates' questions took, and their function in the courtroom in terms of the type of response they elicited. She found that polar (yes/no), disjunctive and WH questions of the type 'what', 'how much' and 'how many' produced minimal responses from the defendants, while only 'how' and 'why' questions required more than a minimal response. This type of question made up only 6 per cent of the total number of questions asked in court hearings. While wary of making claims that correlate form to function directly, Harris concluded that the propositional content of the questions, and their syntactic form in that particular institutional context, resulted in a highly conducive form of questioning by the examining magistrate. Questions included forms such as declaratives which require a yes/no response, 'You're unemployed'; disjunctive questions, 'Are you married or single?'; declarative tag forms such as, 'Everybody else seems to have done something but you, don't they?' or 'You'd better not argue with any foreman in future, had you?'. This type of questioning functioned mainly to obtain information and to accuse, and usually gave rise either to short (yes/no) or minimal answers, confirming the propositional content of the question, or, after a disjunctive question, a restricted choice of answer. Such questioning provided a powerful means of control over the interaction, since defendants were asked to confirm completed propositions rather than introduce their own topics or shape the content of what was discussed. When they started to produce more than minimal responses, they were interrupted by the examining magistrate:

Extract (3)

```
 1. M: um [and what is you - what are your three - your children
 2.    living on - and your wife
 3. D: well I do know they uh receive supplementary benefits sir - I
 4.    realise entirely that it's up to me to counterbalance that
 5.    by paying you [know I know ( )
 6. M:                [are you paying anything at all
 7. D: no I haven't been able to - at all sir - [no I get ( )
 8. M:                                          [are you supporting
 9.    anyone else
10. D: not at all no I live on my own sir
11. M: and how much do you receive then
12. D: fourteen pounds thirty five
13. M: well can't you spare something of that - for your children
14.    - um
15. D: yes - I woul[d do ( )
16. M:             [when did you last pay - anything
```

(Harris, 1984: 15–16)

In cases where defendants did attempt to challenge magistrates or not provide the type of answer required, they were explicitly sanctioned:

Extract (4)

```
1. M: How much do you earn a week
2.    (3.0)
3. D: I don't earn any determinate amount
4.    (2.0)
5. M: hm - well a minimum amount then
6. D: that's my business [isn't it ( )
7. M:                     [no it isn't - it's our business
8.    (7.0)
9. D: I'd say a fair average would be about sixty pound a week
```

(Harris, 1984: 18)

Harris argued that the predominance of this type of conducive questioning in magistrates' courts reinforces the power and status of the examining magistrate in relation to the answering defendant. What these extracts also show is an asymmetry in who can do what in this kind of talk; the magistrates are able not just to do the questioning, but also to determine what counts as an adequate answer, by moving on to the next question and curtailing defendants if necessary, as in lines 6, 8 and 16 in extract (3) above. Although defendants are able to engage in strategies of resistance, as we can see in extract (4), they are ultimately in the position of having to provide answers to magistrates' questions.

FROM INTERACTION TO REPRESENTATION: POWER AND DISCOURSE PRACTICES

Harris's study examined the role of questions, a specific linguistic form, in controlling the talk produced by defendants in magistrates' courts. There has been other research which looks at broader discourse practices within courtroom settings, such as different kinds of evidential accounts and reconstructions of events, which can be more or less congruent with prevailing social and institutional norms and expectations. These studies deal with the representational, rather than the interactional, level of language use, and as such focus on the interface between prevailing commonsense discourses and institutional practices.

Susan Ehrlich (1998) has analysed the reconstruction of sexual consent in a sexual harassment disciplinary tribunal, and the ways in which the defendant represented himself as innocent. In extract (5) below, a tribunal member (GK) is questioning the defendant (MA) about his actions:

Extract (5)

```
 1. GK: I'm trying to gather from this is that you read more verbal
 2.     signals than non-verbal signals
 3.     [and I'm trying and I'm trying to]
 4. MA: [that she likes me?              ]
 5. GK: Yes so that you're paying attention to her, according to your
 6.     testimony, to her non-verbal signals. It is really hard you
 7.     see, the point is when the idea 'no means no' and when
 8.     when people are- tend to give people signals in different
 9.     ways and I'm just trying to interpret for
10.     [myself these signals
11. MA: [Yeah I know there's there's a communication thing.
```

(Ehrlich, 1998: 161)

MA's line of defence was that he misread the complainants' signals that his attention was unwelcome, and this was endorsed by some members of the tribunal who believed that this misinterpretation could arise from communicative differences between men and women. Ehrlich argues that the tribunal was conducted according to a male view of what counts as reasonable resistance to sexual aggression, and that despite both complainants' frequent claims to feelings of fear and humiliation, the lenient treatment of the defendant was based on the view that the resistance of the women concerned had been weak, equivocal and inadequate. Ehrlich claims that underlying the defendant's definition of consent, and the tribunal's decision, is discourse *about* gender differences, the 'deficiency' model of miscommunication:

By characterising the complainants' expressions of resistance as 'deficient' and their behaviour as 'inaction' ... two of the tribunal members did not look beyond a reasonable *man's* own experiences and perceptions to the socially structured differences between women and men that may 'affect whether or not a person [woman] is substantially harmed by particular actions'.   (p. 167)

Another study which focuses on more or less powerful forms of discursive and social practices is John Conley and William O'Barr's (1990) analysis of how self-represented litigants in small claims courts present their evidence. They found that litigants tended to use either 'rule-oriented' or 'relational' accounts; those litigants whose accounts concentrated on issues that the court found easier to handle, that is, the 'theory' of a case, the existence of contracts, obligations and facts relevant to those issues, were more likely to succeed than those whose accounts were centred on motivations, relationships and complex social problems. Conley and O'Barr suggest that a litigant's use of a rule-oriented account 'correlates with exposure to the sources of social power, in particular the literate and rule-based cultures of business and law' (p. 194) and conclude that courts are inherently biased against litigants whose relational accounts are seen as rambling and off the point.

Both Ehrlich and Conley and O'Barr relate these discursive differences in courtroom accounts, through which speakers represent and reconstruct events according to different views of the world, to broader social differences where some ways of talking about events can be more powerful than others. In the cases above, the male-oriented view of what constitutes reasonable resistance, and the legal, rule-oriented view of what constitutes reasonable evidence, marginalise or discount other reconstructions of events seen from a different perspective.

POWER AS 'TERRITORY': GAINING ACCESS TO DISCURSIVE SPACE

The issue of who gets to talk and how much has been a central one in research into the relationship between social status and power in language use. In the field of language and gender, particularly for feminist researchers working within the 'dominance' paradigm,[9] the question of how to approach the analysis of power has always been a live theoretical issue. While there is no widespread agreement on where to locate the manifestation of power in discourse, there is a well-established body of research which has explored a range of linguistic and discursive phenomena in cross-sex interaction. For example, Don Zimmerman and Candace West (1975) looked at the function of interruptions as a powerful device in talk, while Carole Edelsky (1981) examined the differential between women and men in terms of amount of talk and access to the 'floor' as indicators of asymmetrical distribution of social power. This type of approach is based on what I can best describe as a 'territorial' model of power in interaction, where the more turns you can take (or stop other people taking) and the greater your occupation of the floor, the more power you have as a participant in the talk.

Recent research which is based on this 'territorial' conceptualisation of power in discourse is a study by Herring, Johnson and DiBenedetto (1996) on gendered participation in, and contributions to, an academic discussion list on the internet.

Herring, Johnson and DiBenedetto found that despite the potential of the world wide web as an apparently democratic medium for interaction, where indicators of social status and identity are supposedly absent, a gender differential is still endemic in electronic discussion lists. Monitoring the activity on one particular list (MBU, or 'Megabyte University', considered by its users to be more 'friendly and supportive' than some others) for just over one month, they found that for two days during that period, when there were more women contributing to a particular topic in the discussion thread than there were men (contrary to the norm which was 30: 70), this generated a protest from the male contributors. They suggest that 'from the perspective of the men in the group, the women's increased participation was not only unexpected, it also appeared to be more than it actually was' (p. 201). Moreover from a quantitative perspective, this differential matches similar findings in research focusing on talk in other settings (classrooms, meetings, seminars) that the threshold for women's participation in all these activities is between 20 and 30 per cent before men feel that women are starting to dominate the interaction. If power relations and status in this form of communication can be measured in terms of levels of participation and levels of response to postings, then this study not only shows that men respond more frequently to topics introduced by other men than they do to topics introduced by women, but also that women tend to do the same.

POWER AND INTERACTION:
A DIVISION OF LABOUR

Another approach to analysing discursive power has been to consider the accomplishment of interaction as asymmetrically gendered work (Fishman, 1983; Sattel, 1983). In a study of (white, professional, heterosexual) couples talking at home, Pamela Fishman found that the women worked harder than their male partners at maintaining conversations, while being less successful at getting their topics taken up in the talk. The men, on the other hand, while doing much less interactional work, were much more successful in establishing the topics of conversation. This, Fishman claimed, resulted in 'the definition of what is appropriate or inappropriate conversation' becoming the man's choice (1983: 89). Victoria DeFrancisco (1991) found the same pattern recurring in a similar study of interaction between couples in their homes, where the most common violation of conversational turn-taking was 'no response', particularly by the men. Again, evidence from her data showed that, although the women worked harder to maintain interaction, they were less successful than the men. Like Fishman, DeFrancisco concluded that men were relatively silent in domestic interaction and that this as a result silenced the women. Both scholars claimed that this pattern of conversational behaviour results in men defining and controlling 'the day-to-day reality of these couples' communication styles' (DeFrancisco, 1991), while the women did most of the work of generating communication.

These studies are based on a more economic model of discursive power; that is, the unequal division of labour and respective payoffs for those who do the most work (what Fishman termed the 'shitwork' of conversation). From the evidence in these studies, the women's efforts to establish and maintain cross-sex communication meant them having to talk more, but to less effect, than the men. However, there can be a danger in making generalisations about the ineffectiveness of women's talk from one specific domain (domestic relations), where there has traditionally been inequality in the kind of work done by women and men, when other research has shown that within other domains, notably in predominantly single-sex interaction, women's talk can be a powerful and highly effective means of forging and shaping social relationships (Coates, 1996; Nelson, 1988).

TALKING POWERFULLY

Approaching the question of how talk can be powerful from a rather different perspective, Marjorie Goodwin (1990, 1992) has argued that research into women's language needs to move away from mainly white, anglo-saxon-dominated cultural generalisations about what constitutes powerful and powerless talk, and look at what happens in diverse communities in both single-sex and cross-sex talk. In a detailed study of how African American girls organise their social relations through a particular form of talk event, the 'he-said-she-said', Goodwin shows that girls do engage in powerful forms of talk, and this is particularly evident in an activity known as 'instigating'. In this kind of activity, the girls bring about public confrontations between an offending party (a girl who talks about another behind her back) and the injured party through the process of instigating. This involves one girl setting up another by reporting a series of stories about what the offending girl has been saying. The accusation is then made in a typical three-part syntactic form, X said that Y said that Z said:

```
Kerry said you said that (0.6)
I wasn't gonna go around Poplar no more
```

(Goodwin, 1992: 184)

Goodwin argues that power is clearly evident in the activity of instigating, in so far as this creates a situation where confrontation and negotiation between shifting alliances of girls are worked out. She also notes that this occurs at a level of complexity she never observed among the boys in her study, and concludes that to 'investigate power in female speech, one place to begin might be how females use language to orchestrate the important political events in their lives' (p. 194) and that the 'he-said-she-said' is an example of one such political event.

All these studies offer very different methodological approaches to analysing power in interaction in a range of different contexts, and all have important things to say about where and how power gets 'done' in language. Herring, Johnson and DiBenedetto's (1996) analysis shows up interesting asymmetries in cross-sex communication in a new medium along the lines of the 'territorial' model of access to and occupation of discursive space; both Fishman's and DeFranciso's studies of the work of interaction as an asymmetrical division of labour provide the critical edge that is missing in much research based on the 'difference' model of cross-sex communication (for example, Tannen, 1992). In contrast, Goodwin's work suggests that there are ways in which girls' talk can be regarded as powerful in very local, contextually specific forms of interaction.

While they certainly provide different perspectives on the analysis of power in discourse from the point of view of gender, these studies do not necessarily refute each other's findings. Rather, they offer complementary approaches to the multifaceted phenomenon of power in a range of contexts. So, although the territorial model of power may seem to conflict with the economic one, in so far as 'talking more' has been treated, rather contradictorily, as both a powerful and a powerless activity, the key to that contradiction is to be found in the discursive context and relative status of the participants. Talk in the context of private domestic relations is a very different activity from talk in the public domain, in terms of the communicative work that is going on, what that talk means to those involved in it and the roles that can be taken up within it.

POWER, INTERACTION AND BUILDING SOCIAL HIERARCHIES

To conclude this section I want to look at two further studies which have attempted to show how discursive power works on a local level in interaction. Again, they are from very different methodological paradigms, yet they share a basic claim: that hierarchy and status are actively established through talk rather than being static social categories.

In an analysis of power and status in the talk between trainers and trainees in a Swiss institute of psychotherapy (which she describes as a small, close-knit social network, or 'community of the mind'), Julie Diamond (1996) claims that there are two kinds of rank that speakers can occupy in talk: institutional rank and local rank. She questions the assumption made in many studies of institutional interaction that power is a property of speakers who hold higher institutional rank, and argues for a view of power in discursive interaction as political and consensual; in other words, as the ability of a speaker to get his or her interpretation accepted by other speakers. This ability is contested and negotiated in discourse primarily through the work of raising topics in talk, which are then accepted or rejected by other participants.

Diamond is critical of the notion that turns at talk are the economic unit of discourse: 'if we assume that in conversation people have things to say, then the currency of conversation consists of ideas or statements rather than turns' (p. 94). She bases her analysis of the work speakers do to get topics raised and accepted on speech–act theory and 'face' in politeness theory (Brown and Levinson, 1987) rather than on the turn-taking model of conversation used, for example, by Zimmerman and West (1975). Diamond claims that getting a topic raised successfully is a powerful discursive action, as is forcing another speaker to go 'on-record' by rejecting a topic, regardless of a speaker's institutional status. However, the attempt to raise a topic is also a risky, potentially face-threatening action for speakers to undertake, and people engage in a range of strategies in raising, ratifying, rejecting and withdrawing topics in conversation. Typically, she found that high-rank members use 'solidarity' politeness, while low-rank members use 'defence' politeness (Scollon and Scollon, 1981).

As an example of the work that goes on around raising topics in talk, Diamond gives an extract where three women are discussing how to organise a party for new students to the institute:

Extract (6)

```
1. Sylvia: You know, (2.4) one idea of mine, (.) was uh (1.2) to
2.         like hire a band
3.         (1.7)
4. Wendy:  That'd be great
5. Kim:    That's an in[teresting   idea          ]
6. Sylvia:             [do you think that'd be good?] One of
7.         my neighbours, y'know, Monika, she sings in a band
```

(Diamond, 1996: 99)

Here, Diamond suggests that Sylvia's prompt for more acknowledgement from the other participants (line 6) is a result of insecurity about her 'band' topic after the 1.7 second pause in line 3. This pause is long enough to indicate that the other two have not immediately accepted her idea, so she tries to get them to produce a clearer, less-equivocal response to it.

While this study is interesting in its focus on power as a micro-level, interactive phenomenon, and in the way that it questions *a priori* judgements about what constitutes discursive power, it still leaves questions open about the relationship between institutional and local rank, and about the work that speakers are doing to maintain these in this context. Firstly, if higher-ranking speakers use different kinds of strategies to get topics raised or rejected than lower-rank speakers, then this may be a way of maintaining existing power relations, while masking those relations through 'solidarity' politeness strategies. This would support Fairclough's (1992) claim that the move to 'conversationalise' public discourse masks underlying relations of power. Secondly, the notion of 'topic' as the currency for talk may hold in certain contexts, such as meetings, task-oriented working groups and the like that constitute Diamond's corpus, but may not be so useful in others, where different kinds of activities may be going on. Furthermore, the claim that discursive power is political on the level of getting your topics ratified by others, still does not account for the many other kinds of social relations and actions that are being accomplished through talk.

As a contrasting example, in their study of arguments and the construction of hierarchy in children's street play, Goodwin and Goodwin (1990) describe how hierarchy is an 'interactional, collaborative achievement' between a group of boys preparing for a sling-shot fight (p. 113). At one stage in their analysis they show how a shift of topic can function to invoke different participation frameworks in the talk (Goffman, 1981). The extract below is an exchange between two brothers, Michael and Huey, the leaders of the two sling-shot teams, and two other boys. Michael (the elder brother) is trying to make Huey pick his team and get ready to fight, but Huey resists:

Extract (7)

```
1. Michael: All right who's on your side Huey
2. Chopper: Pick- pick four people
3. Huey:    It's quarter to four and I'm not
4.          ready to go yet
5. Bruce:   Me neither.
6. Huey:    I'm not going till four thirty.
7. Michael: Well get in there and get them papers
8.          off that couch [before
```

(Goodwin and Goodwin, 1990: 111)

They argue that by shifting the topic from the fight to household chores (line 7) Michael is not only able to continue to make demands on Huey, but is also able to exclude Chopper and Bruce by invoking an activity domain that does not involve them: 'By virtue of its ability to invoke alternative situated activity systems, topic provides parties to a conversation with resources for rapidly changing how they are aligned to each other, and the activities that are relevant at that moment' (p. 112). So the view of topic as simply content (what gets talked about) to a large extent ignores the powerful interactive work that can go on around topic shifts in talk in terms of changing participation frameworks, excluding some participants and realigning the relationships between others.

WHEN POWER IS NOT TALKING

Susan Gal (1992) has pointed out that there has been a tendency to define powerful or powerless talk by attributing types of discursive actions directly to speaker identities, whereas in practice these actions have culturally (and probably even situationally) determined status. Taking the example of silence, Gal reminds us that, while western feminist scholars have taken women's silence to be 'a result and symbol of passivity and powerlessness'(p. 154), in some institutional settings (interviews, police examinations, religious confession) silence can be a resource for the institutionally more powerful participants. It can also equally well be a form of resistance and protest (Gal cites its use by Western Apache men to disconcert white outsiders, and by seventeenth-century English Quakers who refused to speak when expected to do so to mark their ideological commitment).

The following anecdote illustrates how silence can function as a powerful resource in interaction. It is a personal story told by a male, mature student about his experience as a candidate in an interview for a master's degree in the social sciences. On entering the office of the (male) member of staff interviewing him, he was greeted and asked to sit down. There then followed a long silence which he described as lasting several minutes (although it may actually have been much shorter than this, his experience of it as 'long' is the important point) before the interviewer asked him a question on a subject he knew absolutely nothing about. However, rather than responding straight away, the candidate deliberately remained silent, while the interviewer made several attempts to prompt him to say something. Eventually, his reply went something like this: 'you took five minutes to formulate that question, you could at least give me the same amount of time to formulate an answer'. After waiting for a little longer, he then added: 'I know nothing at all about that.'

The interviewer's initial silence in this context had been perceived and described by the candidate interviewee as a display of power, as interactive behaviour that was hostile and which he felt was clearly designed to disconcert him in what was already a potentially very stressful situation. But for various reasons (a significant one probably being that this particular candidate was a mature student with several years experience of work behind him) he was able to respond to the interviewer's use of silence in a way that challenged the asymmetrical character of the interview and succeeded in establishing the talk on a more equal footing between them.[10]

So it is perhaps more useful to consider certain kinds of discursive actions, including silence, as interactional *resources* available to speakers across many different settings, than to see particular forms of utterances as being inherently more or less powerful than others. Which of the resources a speaker chooses to use, and the interactional outcomes of that choice, will depend on any number of factors at play in the context of the talk at hand. This will always be an 'of the moment' affair; power cannot necessarily always be read off from quantitative differences in the use of linguistic forms, nor from fixed categories of more or less powerful forms of speech. However, what speakers can do with these resources needs to be considered within the institutional context of the talk, which sets up positions for people to talk from, and affects the kind of actions speakers can effectively accomplish from within those positions.

ANALYSING POWER – WHAT NEXT?

In this chapter I have discussed a range of different approaches to the analysis of power in talk, from the macro-level of Fairclough's view of discourse as a social and discursive practice to the micro-level work on empirical data which characterises CA through a range of studies which have drawn on various methods of analysis and conceptualisations of power. On the one hand, it is clear that CDA needs to pay closer attention to the details of talk so as to better understand discursive power as a local, interactive phenomenon. On the other, these details need to be situated contextually, since what participants in institutional interaction (and arguably in any occasion for talk) get to say, and what the interactional consequences turn out to be, is shaped by their roles and identities within a given context.[11] In other words, power in discourse is more than simply a question of the relationship between one turn and the next, although that relationship is a significant one. What happens between one turn and the next also depends on the rights and obligations which accrue to speakers' relative contextual status, and what counts as powerful from a discursive point of view, as we have seen in the studies above, will be an outcome of the environment within which a stretch of talk occurs, as well as an outcome of the participants' actions within their turns at talk.

To draw an analogy with the traditional duality in approaches to the study of language, analysing power in discourse has to be both a diachronic and a synchronic process. To the sequential, moment-by-moment analysis of talk as it unfolds in any interaction we need to add a 'historical' dimension. That is, a way of analysing how the outcomes of a turn at talk as discursive action may be shaped by the context in which it occurs, as one instance of talk in what may be institutionally an ongoing set of sequences of similar kinds of talk. Hugh Mehan (1991) has pointed out that participants in a talk event have 'discourse identities' which create differentials in terms of who does what kind of action (for example, requester and request granter, complainer and complaint receiver). Similarly, there are differentials in discourse identities which are institutionally constructed, whether they are doctor and patient, interviewer and interviewee, police officer and suspect, or host and caller in a radio show. These identities may on one level be synchronic, in the sense that they are talked into being, in and of the moment, and recursively so, but they also pre-exist that moment, in the sense that participants involved in these contexts for talk have diachronically constructed identities which are already socially, professionally or otherwise situationally defined.

Participants normally bring to all talk events some set of conventionally structured knowledge about the kind of talk they are engaged in, and what their role is in that context. As competent members of a culture, or of a speech community, we do not only produce talk, but we can usually recognise what kind of talk is going on, without necessarily being an active participant in it. We distinguish between different linguistic registers, between different speech genres and events; we recognise an argument, a story, a political interview, a court case for what it is; we know who typically does what in different contexts for talk. As participants in a conversation, we make sense of what we are doing, not just in terms of orienting to the previous speaker's utterance, turn, gesture or whatever, but also in terms of what that utterance or turn is doing at a particular moment in a particular context. These assumptions may not always be made explicit; they may, or may not, emerge in the unfolding talk, and may or may not be visible to an analyst in that form, but without them it is difficult to imagine how much of the day-to-day business of talk would get done. Indeed, the routine conduct of any form of interaction is frequently only made salient by breaches of that conduct, at times when participants break from the unmarked, conventional patterns of talk either to do something different, to challenge or resist a particular action or to engage in repairing a breach that has occurred. In other words, one way that we often become aware of a normative pattern in interaction, and of its conventional, contextual shape is by noticing a change, or disruption, to that pattern.

If discursive power functions broadly as a way of maintaining existing social relations, on the one hand, and as a local, negotiated and relatively shifting phenomenon, on the other, we need to understand how it works both in the fine-grained detail of local interaction, as well as in the conventions and norms of social discursive practices. Harris (1995) has suggested that any study of empirical data in institutional contexts should be based on four components: propositional, intertextual, contextual/historical and interactional. Much of the research in the critical discourse tradition, for example the critical study of racist discourse (van Dijk, 1991, 1993; Wodak, 1993, 1996), is more at home when dealing with the first three components, rather than with the interactional level of language, while conversation analysis has fought shy of bringing issues of context and power into the interactional arena (although see my discussion of Hutchby, 1996a, 1996b; and Silverman, 1997 above).

The approach to power that I am taking here, as a discursive phenomenon constantly in play in talk, involves careful attention to what constitutes power 'at its extremities' (Foucault, 1980: 96). This means looking in detail at the kinds of things that speakers do at a very local level, such as the organisation of turn-taking sequences, occupation of particular kinds of turn positions, and the accomplishment of certain kinds of conversational actions. Drawing on Foucault's concept of power as existing in a complex and shifting web of social relationships and actions, the local detail of interaction is one place where the intricate weaving of that web can be best observed and analysed. However, discursive power is also a contextually produced, and contextually relative, phenomenon. By this I mean that speakers' access to particular kinds of positions in talk, and the practical outcomes of discursive resources they might have available to them, will to a large extent be shaped by the institutional context they are talking in, and will not always be the same across contexts. Any detailed analysis of power in interaction therefore needs to be informed by an account of context, the social relationships it sets up between participants, and speakers' rights and obligations in relation to their discursive and institutional roles and identities.

The following chapters in this book contain analyses, in the form of case studies, of different kinds of talk between participants in different institutional settings. In each case, I give a detailed account of how the talk is organised on a local level, but also an account of how it is shaped by the institutional context in which it occurs. In so doing, my aim is to provide a deeper perspective into the relationship between power and discourse, and what this relationship produces on an interactional level in terms of how speakers construct and negotiate more or less powerful positions in situated, asymmetrical encounters for talk.

NOTES

1. This is the distinction first given by Saussure in the 'Cours de Linguistique Generale' (1922) between language as a system ('langue') and language in use ('parole').
2. Fairclough has pointed out that 'one cannot simply apply Foucault's work in discourse analysis'; it is rather a matter of 'trying to operationalise his insights in actual methods of analysis' (1992: 38).
3. This criticism has been particularly relevant to feminist debates about language, and the view that patriarchal systems of meaning prevent women from expressing themselves fully and effectively, thus contributing to the maintenance of a dominant male view of the world (Spender, 1980). Although Spender's strongly deterministic point of view has been questioned by other feminists (cf. Black and Coward, 1981; Cameron, 1985), her theory that language upholds a notion of male superiority which makes patriarchy seem natural and fair remains central to the feminist critique of language (Cameron, 1985).
4. Talk is a jointly constructed interactive 'here and now' affair, while texts, although they can have 'interactive' qualities (letters, notes passed in class) with interpersonal aspects (direct address, an of the moment recipient), are a very different kind of 'planned' discourse.

5. For a detailed discussion of interactional asymmetries in discourse, see Drew and Heritage (1992).
6. Fairclough bases his analytic framework on the exchange structure model of Sinclair and Coulthard (1975).
7. I offer this interpretation on the basis of the transcript only, as I do not have access to the original data tape.
8. In a similar vein, Victoria deFrancisco (1991) notes a comment made by Anita Pomerantz (1989), that without bridging the gap between analyses of conversation and issues which are socially relevant to participants, then such analyses do little to inform the political realities of people's lives.
9. Cameron (1997) provides a succinct account of the difference/dominance debate in feminist linguistic research.
10. This story was told to me first hand by the student concerned. After the interview, he was offered a place on the course.
11. Margaret Wetherell (1998) has noted in relation to discourse analysis in the field of social psychology that, although CA offers a useful technical approach to the analysis of interaction, it cannot always provide an adequate answer to its own question 'why that utterance here?'.

3

◆

INSTITUTIONAL DISCOURSE AS ASYMMETRICAL TALK: POWER AND ORDERLY INTERACTION IN A POLICE INTERVIEW

In this chapter I develop the discussion of power in talk from the perspective of orderliness in institutional discourse. What is it that underlies the order of institutional exchanges, or, in other words, the organisation of interaction in institutional talk? There are two important theoretical claims about order that have been made in critical discourse analyses of institutional talk: the first claim is that orderliness in interactive sequences of talk is dependent on commonsense structures of background knowledge,[1] and the second is that institutionally determined social roles produce dominant and subordinate positions which affect the rights and obligations of speakers (Fairclough, 1989, 1995). However, although shared commonsense background knowledge can produce ideological coherence in some stretches of talk between some participants, it does not of itself create interactive order, and in this chapter I show how the 'orderliness' of talk is accomplished by the participants in it, rather than pre-existing as a set of shared assumptions about what constitutes orderly discursive behaviour. I will also show (in support of the second claim) how close attention to the detail of talk can reveal a great deal more about the interactive work speakers do to take up, establish and maintain discursive positions in talk, than critical discourse analysis has tended to assume. My data are taken from a police interview with a woman who is making a complaint of rape, which was recorded during the filming of a television documentary.

Fairclough (1995, 1992) has suggested that discursive norms of interaction are shaped and defined by what he terms *ideological discourse formations*; specifically, that the 'orderliness' of discursive interaction depends on shared background knowledge which is ideologically motivated, but which often appears as 'naturalised' or as 'commonsense' to the participants involved. Speakers participate in talk events according to mutual recognition of rules and conventions of the event which they hold as commonsense, or 'naturalised' ideologies,[2] which he explains as follows:

> When I refer to the 'orderliness' of an interaction, I mean the feeling of participants in it (which may be more or less successfully elicited or inferred from their interactive behaviour) that things are as they should be, i.e. as one would normally expect them to be.   (1995: 28)

According to this definition, orderliness is characterised by the sense of the participants that things are proceeding 'normally', a sense which is evident from the coherence of interaction, meaningful turn taking, and generally appropriate and expected discursive behaviour from the participants' perspective. As an example of this type of conventionalised discursive behaviour, Fairclough gives the following exchange between a doctor and a medical student, which takes place in a neo-natal unit:

Extract (1)

```
 1. S: well here's a young baby boy . who we've decided is .
 2.    thirty . seven weeks old now . was born . two weeks
 3.    ago . um is fairly active . his eyes are open . he's
 4.    got hair on . his head [. his eyes are [open
 5. D:                        [yes           [yes you've
 6.    told me that
 7. S: um he's crying or [making
 8. D:                   [yeah we we we we've heard
 9.    that now what other examination are you going to make
10.    I mean [---]
11. S: erm we'll see if he'll respond to
12. D:                              now look did we not
13.    look at a baby with a head problem yesterday .
14. S: right
```

(Transcript from Fairclough, 1989: 44)

In this extract there is an asymmetrical relationship between the doctor and the student. The doctor, as the more powerful participant, 'controls' the actions of the student through interruptions, questions and directives, while the student is in the less powerful position of having to answer and comply (Fairclough, 1989: 46). This control, Fairclough argues, is a result of the conventions and constraints of the discourse type; in this case, the kind of talk that typically and commonsensically goes on between doctors and medical students.

However, the notion of order in talk as a sense that things are 'as one would normally expect them to be', which can be inferred from speakers' interactive behaviour, is a rather problematic gauge for the evaluation of orderliness. How is this sense that 'things are as they should be' to be measured? Fairclough has suggested that talk can be seen as orderly in the coherence of interaction between participants, 'smooth' turn taking, the use of appropriate social markers of deference, an appropriate register and so on. From this it would follow that 'dis-orderly' talk might involve incoherence across speaker turns, constant interruptions and disruption of turn-taking sequences, inappropriate register and inappropriate use of deference markers.

In the following discussion of a particular instance of institutional interaction, I want to take a rather different approach to the question of orderliness in talk, which I sketch out briefly here before turning to the data. I argue that interaction can still be shown to be orderly, even when speakers interrupt each other, vie for the floor or use inappropriate registers, and that order is not necessarily determined by underlying background assumptions about 'the way things should be' that are shared by all participants in the talk. Speakers interact within a system of turns and exchange sequences, whether they are engaging in a straightforward conversation, an argument or some form of dispute or disagreement. Even in fictional dialogue, such as we might find in a play by Tom Stoppard or Harold Pinter, where normal expectations of coherence and meaning are often disrupted, and communication fails spectacularly, the orderliness of the discursive structure is not affected. All talk is accomplished jointly within an interactive context, but this does not mean that speakers need necessarily share the same assumptions about the world, that is, the same naturalised commonsense background knowledge, in order to produce recognisably coherent sequences of talk.

It is usually the case that matters which become problematic or 'disorderly' in conversation, and which lead to misunderstandings between speakers, tend to be dealt with in repair sequences as they occur. Schegloff, Jefferson and Sacks (1977) have described how speakers attend to procedural problems in turn taking (for instance, what happens when overlapping talk is produced by two speakers self selecting as next speaker) and how problems of meaning, which arise during the course of a stretch of talk, get resolved. However, I take it (as Fairclough does) that speakers do have sets of beliefs or assumptions that we can call background knowledge (ideological or otherwise), which may shape their talk and which will sometimes get to be explicitly displayed in what they say. However, I prefer to use the terms *ideological coherence* to refer to the unifying premises, which can be shown to underlie the discourse of a speaker from a representational perspective, and *orderliness* to refer to norms of conversational interaction, that is turn-taking sequences, adjacency pairs and the like, through which speakers engage in talk.

Let us now turn to the data to illustrate how this distinction might work in practice. In this analysis of a police interview with a woman making a complaint of rape,[3] I show how the interaction can be seen as orderly in terms of what the speakers are doing, but that this orderliness in the talk does not necessarily depend on the speakers' sharing the same background knowledge. An account of the power relations in this talk, and of the asymmetrical nature of the interaction in terms of the participants' institutional status, can be approached from a rather different angle than that suggested by Fairclough (1995). Rather than assuming a corresponding mapping of institutional context and a dominant ideological discourse formation, there can be conflicting discourses at work in any instance of asymmetrical institutional talk, and these conflicts get to be played out within the orderly organisation of speaker turns at talk, as we will see.

ORDERLINESS AND DISCURSIVE STRUCTURE

Extract (2) below is quite a long sequence from an interview which takes place in a police station between a woman (designated as A) who has come to make a complaint of rape, and two male police officers (B and C). This particular stretch of talk is taken from towards the end of the interview, but I will also be referring to earlier sections later on in the analysis. Prior to the talk in this sequence, a third police interviewer (D) has also been present, but he leaves the room half way through the interview. The participant framework of two (and at one point three) interviewers and one interviewee is inherently asymmetrical, as is the gender distribution: three men, one woman. In my discussion of these data, I focus on how this talk can be accounted for as orderly in terms of their sequential organisation, and coherent with regard to the ideological assumptions underlying the talk of each participant, yet with clear evidence of conflicting assumptions between the participants.

Extract (2)

```
 1. C: you do realise that when we have you medically examined
 2.    (1.4)
 3. C: and=
 4. B:    =they'll come up with nothing=
 5. C:                        =the swabs (.) are taken
 6.    (1.0)
 7.    it'll show (.)if you've had sexual intercourse with three
 8.    men this afternoon it'll [show
 9. A:                        [it'll show each one
10. C: it'll [show each one
11. B:       [hmm
12. A: yeah I [know that
13. B:        [alright (.) so=
14. A:                 =so it would show [(xxx)
15. C:                                  [it'll confirm
16.    that you've had sex=
17. B:                    =hmm=
18. C:                       =or not(.)with three men (.)
19.    alright so we can confirm it's happened (.) that you've
20.    had sex with three men (.) if it does confirm it (.) then
21.    I would go as far as to say (.) that you went to that
22.    house willingly (1.4) there's no struggle (.) you could
23.    have run away quite easily (.) when you got out of the car
24.    (.) to go to the house (.) you could have got away quite
25.    easily (.) you're well known (.) in Reading (.)to the
26.    uniformed(.)lads (.) for being a nuisance in the streets
27.    shouting and bawling (.) coupla times you've been
28.    arrested (.) f- under the mental health act (1.0) for
29.    shouting and screaming in the street (1.0) haven't ya
30.    (1.9)
31. A: when I was ill yeah=
32. C:                    =yeah right (.) so (.) what's to stop
33.    you (.) shouting and screaming (.) in the street (.) when
34.    you think you're gonna get raped (1.9) you're not
```

```
35.    frightened at all you walk in there (.) quite blasé
36.    you're not frightened at all
37.    (1.0)
38. A: I was frightened=
39. C:                  =you weren't (1.2) you're showing no
40.    signs of emotion every now and again you have a little
41.    tear
42.    (2.0)
43. B: (xxx) if you were frightened (1.0) and you came at me I
44.    think I would dive (.) I wouldn't take you on
45.    (2.3)
46. C: you don't fool [(anybody)
47. B:                [you'd (take xxx)
48. C: you don't fool [(xxx)
49. A:                [why would I frighten [you (xxx )   ]
50. B:                                      [you you (jus-)]
51.    only a little (wife)
52. B: it doesn't matter (.) you're female and you've probably
53.    got a hell of a temper (.) if you were to go=
54. A:                                       =I haven't
55.    got a temper [(xxx) a hell of a temper
56. C:              [(oh I dunno)
57. B: I think if things if if things were up against a a wall
58.    (.) I think you'd fight and you'd fight very hard
```

Let us start by looking at the orderliness of the organisation of speaker turns in this extract, focusing to begin with on the first 18 lines. In line 1 of the transcript, C's question to A about the outcome of a medical examination 'you do realise . . .', is the first part of an adjacency pair (Sacks, Schegloff and Jefferson, 1974) to which A eventually produces an answering second part in line 12 'yeah I know'. So despite the intervening turns, C's question gets an answer. In between this adjacency pair, some things happen which appear to be very orderly actions. There is a form of insertion sequence (Levinson, 1983) in lines 9 and 10 where A interrupts C by offering a candidate completion of his utterance 'it'll show each one', which he then confirms with a repeat:

Extract (2.a)

```
 7. C:    it'll show (.)if you've had sexual intercourse with three
 8.       men this afternoon it'll [show
 9. A: →                          [it'll show each one
10. C: → it'll [show each one
11. B:         [hmm
12. A:    yeah I [know that
13. B:           [alright (.) so=
```

So it seems that there is some kind of agreement being established here between A and C about what the outcome of the examination will be.

In extract 2, B's contributions to the talk, the first one coming straight after C's continuing 'and' in line 3 after the 1.4 second pause, and the second when he overlaps C in line 9, are also highly orderly. When C pauses at the end of his utterance in line 1 (containing the subordinate clause 'when we have you medically examined'), B takes the next turn and completes it for him syntactically with a main clause 'they'll come up with nothing', thereby giving his view of the outcome of the examination. As we have seen, what happens next is the apparent display of agreement between A and C about a slightly different outcome, 'it'll show each one'. But B challenges this by producing a sceptical 'hmm' in line 11, overlapping with C, just at the moment where he can be heard to confirm A's understanding that 'it will show each one'. Despite the potential problem of selecting who speaks next in a multi-party situation like this, B's talk is precisely placed at points where it sounds as though A might suppose that C shared the same view as she does about the outcome of a medical examination. The talk produced in this sequence by all three participants is therefore both orderly and cohesive on a turn-by-turn basis.

The same orderliness can be seen in the other exchanges in this stretch of talk, detailed below in extracts (2b–d):

Extract (2.b)

```
27. C: [---] coupla times you've been
28.    arrested (.) f- under the mental health act (1.0) for
29.    shouting and screaming in the street (1.0) haven't ya
30.    (1.9)
31. A: when I was ill yeah=
32. C:                    =yeah right
```

Extract (2.c)

```
34. C: [---] you're not
35.    frightened at all you walk in there (.) quite blasé
36.    you're not frightened at all
37.    (1.0)
38. A: I was frightened=
39. C:                  =you weren't (1.2)
```

Extract (2.d)

```
43. B: (xxx) if you were frightened (1.0) and you came at me I
44.    think I would dive (.) I wouldn't take you on
45.    (2.3)
46. C: you don't fool [(anybody)
47. B:                [you'd (take xxx)
48. C: you don't fool [(xxx)
49. A:                [why would I frighten [you (xxx )    ]
50. B:                                      [you you (jus-)]
51.    only a little (wife)
52. B: it doesn't matter (.) [---]
```

These sequences can be seen as orderly and coherent in the sense that speakers are taking their turns appropriately in response to a prior utterance. For example, in extract (2.b) A's response to C's declarative tag question 'coupla times you've been arrested, haven't ya?' is a qualified confirmation 'when I was ill yeah'. There is also a long gap of nearly two seconds preceding her response. Such a gap is a typical indication that a dispreferred response is coming up in the next turn (Pomerantz, 1984) and A's production of a reason for her arrest, rather than just a straight confirmation, conforms to this pattern. There is also a one second pause after interviewer C's accusatory claim that she wasn't frightened. This too indicates that a dispreferred next action is upcoming in the response, and A does then refute C's claim 'I was frightened'. Later on in the same sequence (extract (2.d)) interviewer B claims that he would be frightened by her. There is then a long pause before interviewer C takes the next turn, which seems to be in support of B's claim about A being a frightening person: 'you don't fool (xxx)'. A's response to these claims: 'why would I frighten you?', occurs in overlap with C, but is nevertheless placed at an appropriate moment as a challenge to the double accusation from the two policemen. So at this point the talk is orderly, even though there is a clear sense that for A matters are not at all 'as they should be'.

IDEOLOGICAL COHERENCE

A long stretch of the talk I have been discussing here, from lines 21–36, consists primarily of police interviewer C constructing an alternative account of what has happened to A. She refutes the evidence on which he bases this account at three points: firstly, by giving a justification for her arrest; secondly, by asserting that she was frightened; and, thirdly, by questioning their claim that she is a frightening person. At each of these moments in the sequence, the interaction follows predictable patterns. There are a series of paired actions: a request for confirmation followed by a mitigated confirmation; an assertion followed by a denial; an accusatory claim followed by a refutation. In terms of its structure, then, and the actions of the participants, the talk can be said to be organised and orderly. However, in attending to the interactional organisation of the talk, we have left to one side the question of coherence in utterance content across participant turns, and it is much less clear that the talk is conducted according to shared background assumptions between the participants.

In a previous analysis of this data extract, Fairclough claimed that 'the most striking instance of ideologically based coherence in this text' is 'you're female and you've probably got a hell of a temper' (1995: 30). In focusing on this utterance for his discussion of mutually assumed commonsense knowledge, however, he seems not to have taken account of A's utterances, but concentrated only on B and C's contributions to the talk. The talk can be considered as coherent according to the criteria of shared background knowledge only with regard to the police interviewers' utterances, not with regard to the woman complainant.

A's utterance (line 31 in extract (2.b)) 'when I was ill yeah' is a qualifying confirmation in response to C's declarative tag question in lines 27–29. In this utterance she implies that not only were there mitigating circumstances for her arrest, but also that she is not ill now. In extract (2.c) A denies C's assertion that she was not frightened, and in extract (2.d) there is a complex exchange involving all three participants, where A questions the notion that she could be frightening and denies that she has a temper (lines 54–5). It is only in extract (2.a) that A could be said to show some agreement with C, but this does not necessarily indicate any shared background assumptions, as the ensuing talk seems to suggest.

So, although we can see this talk as orderly, its order has little to do with shared background assumptions. Rather, at issue in the talk is a whole set of conflicting assumptions about A: the reasons for her previous arrest, whether she was frightened or not and whether she has a temper. From what the interviewers say, they are making explicit the following set of assumptions about the woman A:

She has been arrested before.
She screams and shouts in the street.
She is a frightening person.
She has a temper.

A, on the other hand, holds a set of conflicting assumptions which emerge in the talk as she challenges the claims B and C make about her:

She was arrested (for screaming and shouting) because she was ill.
She was frightened by the three men who attacked her.
She is not a frightening person.
She does not have a temper.

Underlying B and C's utterances seem to be some assumptions that they hold about A in particular and about women in general, but there is no evidence that A shares any of these, rather the opposite. For instance, there is a clear indication that she does not share the assumption that she could frighten a policeman, as her question: 'why would I frighten you?' is the only real information-seeking question in the sequence here. In other parts of the interview, the police questions are frequently requests for confirmation about what Labov and Fanshel (1977) described as 'B events', 'if A makes a statement about B events, then it is heard as a request for confirmation' (p. 100). These questions are not only conducive in the sense that the preferred response is a confirmation of the proposition they contain (Harris, 1984), but they also function as accusations by referring to A's past behaviour in relation to her present complaint (Atkinson and Drew, 1979). I will return to the accusatory nature of the police interviewers' talk in more detail below, but first I want to explore in more detail the underlying discursive coherence of what the three participants say.

As I have just suggested, there are several background assumptions recoverable from B and C's talk that A does not seem to share. From the evidence in what she says and does in her talk, particularly in her questions and challenges to the police interviewers, she appears to be working with a different set of assumptions altogether. At the start of extract (2), C begins his explanation of what the results of the medical examination will show. B and C produce two utterances which are not only syntactically cohesive, as we noted above, but also coherent in terms of their propositional content:

Extract (2.e)

```
1. C: you do realise that when we have you medically examined
2.     (1.4)
3. C: and=
4. B:    =they'll come up with nothing=
5. C:                              =the swabs (.) are taken
6.     (1.0
7.     it'll show (.)if you've had sexual intercourse with three
8.     men this afternoon it'll [show
```

In saying 'they'll come up with nothing' and 'it'll show if you've had sexual inter-course with three men this afternoon', both B and C are implying that medical evidence of rape will not be found. That they are in a position to make these assertions at all is bound up with their institutional status as policemen, rather than their knowledge of medical examinations, and is based to a large extent on their assessment of the woman A as unreliable and mentally unstable. This coherence holds across two participant turns, again indicating that they are working with the same background assumptions, based on the contextual information they have about her. All three police interviewers construct their position from the same perspective: that, although she may have had sex with three men, she has not really been raped.

It is possible that what the policemen are engaging in here is an enactment of a hostile cross-examination of the type that A would encounter in a courtroom situation, with B and C taking up the position of the defence counsel in a rape trial. In fact, earlier in the interview, the third interviewer D had been questioning her about her personal history and recent sexual activity. Before leaving the room, he explicitly stated that if she pressed charges and went to court, she would have to answer all kinds of unpleasant questions of the type he had just been asking.

One striking similarity between the police questioning and courtroom cross examination is that the series of assertions made by the police interviewers about A's actions seem to be clearly 'blame implicative'. In cases of alleged rape, this is a frequent occurrence, where 'questioning to the "victim" can be designed to impugn her action by attempting to show that it was partly or wholly responsible for the defendant's action' (Atkinson and Drew, 1979: 105). In the course of the interview, B and C imply that whatever happened to her was her own fault, since she could have done something to avoid it. C's account of the events makes this explicit:

Extract (2.f)

```
20. C: (>>>) if it does confirm it (.) then
21.    I would go as far as to say (.) that you went to that
22.    house willingly (1.4) there's no struggle (.) you could
23.    have run away quite easily (.)when you got out of the car
24.    (.) to go to the house (.) you could have got away quite
25.    easily
```

A's failure to struggle or run away is interpreted as being indicative of her complicity in the events of the afternoon.

Whatever may be being played out in the talk here, two main observations can be made about the stretch of talk in this extract. First, there is clear evidence of discursively represented ideological coherence between the police interviewers, but not between all three participants. Second, despite this lack of shared ideological coherence between the woman complainant and the policemen, the sequence is nonetheless orderly in so far as all the participants engage in meaningful turn sequences and pairs of conversational actions. Thus it would seem that the mutual recognition of ideologically represented background knowledge is not a precondition of orderliness in discursive interaction. If we are to explore how power relations are manifested in asymmetrical speech encounters, and how they are accomplished discursively, I suggest that we need to pay closer attention to the details of the talk, rather than simply viewing power in talk as the inevitable product of a dominant/subordinate social relationship, and to the underlying structures of ideological coherence which are common to all participants.

FROM ORDERLINESS TO CONTROL

Having addressed some of the issues raised by these data regarding the relationship between power, discourse and orderly talk, I now want to turn to more local concerns in this extract, and, in particular, focus on aspects of control in the talk. I have described the encounter between the police interviewers and the complainant as highly asymmetrical. It seems clear from the data that, in this context, the policemen are in the institutionally powerful roles, and that these roles are maintained in and through the talk throughout the interview, despite occasional challenges from A. Furthermore, although the kind of actions typically involved in reporting a crime to the police (for example, describing the circumstances of the crime, answering police questions, making a statement, etc.) all get done during the course of this interview, they are accomplished in such a way that position A, not as the victim of a criminal attack, but almost as a criminal herself. The policemen repeatedly ask A questions about whether her complaint is genuine or not, as we can see illustrated in the following exchange between D and A:

Extract (3)

```
1. D:  → What you're telling us is it the truth
2. A:    course it is I wouldn't be here now would I
```

Whatever A says or does, her complaint is treated with some considerable scepticism throughout by all three of the police interviewers. Firstly, as has already been observed, their mode of questioning is very much accusatory rather than information-seeking, and A is regularly subjected to blame implicative questions as she goes through her account of the attack. In courtroom cross examinations, it has been found that 'action sequences associated with such tasks as challenging or blaming are managed through questions and answers' (Atkinson and Drew, 1979: 105). Similarly, the question and answer pairs in this interview lead up to an implication of blame on the complainant's part:

Extract (4)

```
 1. B:    after all this happened who was the first person you cl-
 2.       complained to about rape
 3. A:    I told my boyfriend
 4. B:    what time did you tell him
 5. A:    when he came home from work
 6. B:    yeah we- what time's that six five four
 7. A:    bout quarter to (.) six
 8. ?:    quarter [to-
 9. B: →          [quarter to six what time did you get away from
10.       these fellas
11. A:    er I've no idea (.) I went into the job centre it
12.       must have been about=
13. D: →                        =(xxx)why didn't you say anything
14.       to somebody in the job centre (.) surely rape
15.       [is-
16. A:    [I just (did)
17. D:    rape is the next th- as far as a woman is concerned
18.       rape is the next thing to death isn't it
```

Here, interviewer B asks A a series of questions (lines 1, 4, 6) which form a set of pre-sequence exchanges to the blame-implicative question in line 13. Having asked for specific information about the time she told her boyfriend about the attack, his repeat of the time 'quarter to six' followed immediately by another question 'what time did you get away from these fellas' hearably constructs the time lapse between the two events as too long. Then, interviewer D interrupts A's answering turn in line 11 before she gets to give a time, with a further blame-implicative question:

Extract (4.a)

```
11. A:    er I've no idea (.) I went into the job centre it
12.       must have been about=
13. D: →                        =(xxx)why didn't you say anything
14.       to somebody in the job centre
```

The type of turns taken by the policemen in extract (5) below largely consist of declarative statements reconstructing events A has reported, which in many cases can also be seen as pre-sequences to blame attribution:

Extract (5)

```
 1. B:    so you went through the actions of looking for a job
 2.       then you came out
 3. A:    yeah (got the bus home)
 4. B:    got got a bus home (.) your boyfriend eventually arrived
 5.       then you tell him
 6. A:    well I I thought about it when I got home I was
 7.       going to ring the police then I thought (.) better of it
 8. B:    mm hmm
 9. A:    I wasn't gonna ring you I thought I'd better
```

```
10. D:  → why didn't you think first of all ((whispered)) oh my god
11.        I've been raped [(xxx)]
12. A:                      [you know I felt] dirty
13. D:     why don't I go (xxx)I must go to the police station
14.     → and report it why didn't you do that
```

In lines 10–14 there are a series of 'why didn't you' questions which explicitly construct A as failing to react appropriately, failing to call the police, and as somehow, as a result, being 'at fault' for not doing those things.

Another form of questioning which can in certain contexts provide a discursive resource for powerful participants to exercise control in talk is the use of tag questions (Cameron, 1989), particularly when they function as conducive questions leading to a preferred confirmation of the proposition they contain (Harris, 1984). Again, we can see examples of this use of tag question forms in the data, illustrated in this sequence taken from extract (2):

Extract (2.g)

```
27. C:  [---] coupla times you've been
28.        arrested (.) f- under the mental health act (1.0) for
29.        shouting and screaming in the street (1.0) haven't ya
30.        (1.9)
31. A:  when I was ill yeah=
32. C:                      =yeah right (.) so (.) what's to stop
33.        you (.) shouting and screaming (.) in the street (.) when
34.        you think you're gonna get raped (1.9) you're not
35.        frightened at all you walk in there (.) quite blasé
36.        you're not frightened at all
```

C's question (lines 27–29) ending in the tag 'haven't ya' is here followed by a long pause, and a confirming response. But it is also a mitigated response: 'when I was ill yeah'. As already observed, in withholding her answer for this long pause, and in giving the following mitigation, A is producing a dispreferred response turn in this sequence. She seems here to be displaying her awareness that her answer to this question may have potentially risky implications in the following talk. Indeed, this question also turns out to be a type of pre-blame question/answer sequence to C's subsequent accusation in line 35 that A's claim about being frightened is untrue. By using these kinds of pre-sequences to blame-implicative questions, the police interviewers are able to continue with their construction of A as a guilty troublemaker rather than as the victim of an attack.

RECONSTRUCTION OF EVENTS

One of the main actions that the police interviewers engage in during this interview is a reconstruction of the events A has reported. Her account of the attack is told back to her by B and C, but from their perspective rather than hers. Again, as Atkinson and Drew have observed, in courtroom settings, these kind of third-party descriptions can also have an accusatory function. In describing a reported action, cross examiners often imply that a 'paired action' might have been taken on the witness's (or defendant's) part; in other words, one action is expected to trigger another, and if that second action is not taken, then it is likely that some attribution of blame will follow (Atkinson and Drew, 1979: 153).

Ehrlich (1998) has noted a similar phenomenon in her study of the proceedings of a date rape tribunal, where the phrase 'reasonable resistance' (to attempted rape) is a gendered concept, framed in terms of a male perspective on what counts as resistance.[4] The expectation of 'paired actions' is identifiable in the following extract from the same context, where GK is a faculty member of the tribunal questioning MA, the defendant:

Extract (6)

```
1. GK: Uh when you left the room, as you left the room several
2.     times, was the lock ever used?
3. MA: The lock was never used=
4. GK:                        =Was the lock ever used when you
5.     were inside the room?
6. MA: The lock was never used.
```

(Ehrlich, 1998: 162).

Later in the proceedings, in questioning the complainant the same tribunal member puts this to her as a series of possible actions she did *not* take 'You never make an attempt to put him on the floor ... to close the door behind him ... or to lock the door' (Ehrlich, 1998: 160).

In the police interview with A, evidence of these expected 'paired' actions surfaces at various points in the talk of the policemen, as we have already seen in the following examples from extract (2):

Extract (2.h)

```
C:                      [---] coupla times you've been
   arrested (.) f- under the mental health act (1.0) for
   shouting and screaming in the street (1.0) haven't ya (1.9)
A: when I was ill yeah=
C:                    =yeah right (.) so (.) what's to stop
   you (.) shouting and screaming (.) in the street (.)
   when you think you're gonna get raped
```

Extract (2.i) .

```
C:         [---] if it does confirm it (.) then
   I would go as far as to say (.) that you went to that house
   willingly (1.4) there's no struggle (.) you could have run away
   quite easily (.)when you got out of the car (.) to go to the
   house (.)you could have got away quite easily (.)
```

In interviewer C's description of A's experience in these two extracts, her actions are characterised as not those that would be normally expected in such circumstances.

According to C, someone who has been forced into a car will struggle and try to get away. Similarly, according to C, someone who has been arrested for shouting in the street on one occasion will shout and scream on any occasion. In each case, the woman has not acted in the expected way, which enables the police interviewer to construct her as being a willing participant in the events of the afternoon rather than the victim of a rape attack.

The same kind of assumptions shape interviewer B's talk in the next extract. Here, though, A does a lot of work to resist B's construction of her as someone who is not really being emotionally affected by what has happened to her:

Extract (7)

```
 1. B: You've told me that you wouldn't be here (.)
 2. A: that's right=
 3. B:                =why not
 4.    (1.9)
 5. A: because it's a lot of-fuss
 6. B: mm
 7. A: and a lot of aggro for (1.5)
 8. B: for wh[at   ]
 9. A:       [some]thing you can get over (.) that you can
10.    accept
11. B: well you're a lot stronger than some women I've met I'm
12.    glad to say (.) 'n I've met some that've been raped and
13.    all sorts of things have happened to them and they think
14.    that their life is crumbling down around their ankles
15.    like a pair of knickers with the elastic gone
16. A: well that's why I've been in ((bleep out))isn't it
17. B: I dunno
18.    (4.0)
19. A: It's exactly why I've been in ([---])
20.    (1.9)
21. A: why do you think I've been in ([---])=
22. B:                                 =doesn't hold
23.    water this does it
24.    (2.7)
25.    I'm not saying it's not true what I'm saying is (1.0)
26.    there's a lot more to this (.) that unfortunately we
27.    will never know the other side o' the story because we
28.    don't know the other three blokes (.) two one or none
29.    whatever the case may be I don't know (.) all we've got
30.    is your side of the story and you're still making a
31.    fairytale out of it
32.    (1.0)
33. A: I'm not making a fairytale out of it
34.    (1.7)
35. B: think you are
```

In this sequence, B does the same kind of 'blame implicative' questioning that we have already seen in the extracts above. He begins with a description of A's statement 'you've told me that you wouldn't be here', which she confirms (line 2). Then, his questions 'why not' (line 3) and 'for what' (line 8) give rise to a set of answers from A which enable him to produce his description of her as being 'stronger than a lot of women'. The talk in lines 1–10 thus functions as an extended pre-sequence to his 'blame implicative' description in lines 11–15: she is not upset by the attack and so is wasting his time by making an unnecessary fuss. However, his crude assessment of her as not being the sort of woman whose life is 'crumbling down around their ankles' as a consequence of rape, is strongly challenged by A. She responds with a declarative tag question, which, as discussed above, can in some cases function as a powerful discursive resource for speakers. As we have already seen in the context of a magistrates court, the preferred response to this kind of question shape is a confirmation of the proposition it contains. B does something rather different:

Extract (7.a)

```
16. A:  → well that's why I've been in (([---])isn't it
17. B:     I dunno
18.        (4.0)
19. A:  → It's exactly why I've been in (([---])
20.        (1.9)
21.     → why do you think I've been in (([---])=
22. B:                                    =doesn't hold
23.        water this does it (2.7)
```

The interviewer B responds to her first question by saying 'I dunno'. There then follows a long four second pause, after which A takes the next turn to make her point by repeating her assertion with an intensifier: 'It's *exactly* why'. After another pause of nearly two seconds, a clear turn transition point that B does not take up, she pursues the point again by reformulating her question even more strongly: 'why do you think I've been in (([---])?'. In his next turn (line 22) B does not respond to her question, but instead shifts the topic to an assessment of whether her story is true or not.

What can be seen in these extracts is the construction of two different accounts of A's story; in one, she is the victim of an attack, in the other, she is a willing participant in the events. Through their blame-implicative questioning, the policemen produce an account of A as unreliable and unstable, while A resists this through some strong challenging actions. However, despite these challenges, A does not have much success in getting answers to her questions, and in the next section I discuss some possible reasons why this is the case.

SHIFTS IN DISCURSIVE POSITIONS

In extract (7), the speaker turns from line 1 to line 10 follow an orderly sequence of assertion/confirmation, and contain two question/answer pairs, where B is in the first turn position as questioner. At line 11, the police interviewer's assessment of A as 'stronger than some women I've met' opens up the possibility for something else to happen in the following turn; that is, for A to take up something other than the position of answerer. This is precisely what she does, through her declarative tag question 'well that's why I've been in (([---]) isn't it?', thereby shifting B into next turn position as answerer. B does produce an answer here, but it is an equivocal one: 'I dunno'. This again gives A the opportunity to stay in her questioner position for two more turns, but the long pause between B's answer (line 17) and A's next turn seems to indicate some uncertainty between speakers about what is going to happen next. What eventually happens is that A first provides a follow-up response to B's equivocal answer 'It's exactly why I've been in ([---])' and when B does not take up his turn, producing a fairly long pause, she asks her question again, but in a more direct format: 'why do you think I've been in ([---])'. In this sequence, A has shifted momentarily into a potentially stronger discursive position as questioner, since questions normally 'require' answers. However, rather than respond to A's challenging question, B's move in his next turn is to shift topic through another declarative tag question: 'doesn't hold water this does it?' In doing so he not only moves back into his dominant position as questioner, but also withholds an answer to A's question. In other words, the usual discursive norm that questions are conventionally followed by answers does not hold here. B is clearly unwilling to pursue the topic introduced by A (the reason for her being a patient in a mental hospital) because it doesn't serve his goal at that point. The purpose of interviewer B's questions is to get A to produce an assessment of rape as 'something you can get over', and thereby provide further evidence for his position that A has not been raped, and should drop her claim. When this strategy backfires, with A responding to his description of women rape victims as one that precisely applies to her, B in effect refuses to take up the interactional role of answerer for the space of more than one turn, and returns to his former accusation that A is making up her story: 'doesn't hold water'; it is a 'fairytale'.

This change in position from answerer to questioner that A accomplishes in the sequence above results in a momentary shift in the power relations between interviewer and interviewee. The type of answer that B gives, and the longer than normal pauses between speaker turns, are two indications that something different is going on at that point in the talk, and I suggest that this constitutes a disruption to the institutional discursive norms of this type of police interview. A similar disruption can be seen in extract (2.d), where again A manages to take up the role of questioner after B has produced an assessment of her as being able to defend herself:

Extract (2.d)

```
43. B:     (xxx) if you were frightened (1.0) and you came at me I
44.        think I would dive (.) I wouldn't take you on
45.        (2.3)
46. C:     you don't fool [(anybody)
47. B:                    [you'd (take xxx)
48. C:     you don't fool [(xxx)
49. A: →                  [why would I frighten [you (xxx )    ]
50. B:                                          [you you (jus-)]
51.        only a little (wife)
52. B:     it doesn't matter (.) [---]
```

This time, rather than manifesting itself through long pauses between speaker turns, the disruption takes the form of more overlapping talk as interviewer B struggles in his temporary role as answerer (line 50). The interaction in terms of next speaker selection is more complex in this sequence as interviewer C is also a co-participant, which may account for the overlapping talk at lines 46/47 between B and C. However, B's utterance at line 50 shows that he begins to produce an answer to A's question, but then stops as she completes her turn (line 51). This gives him the possibility to repair his prospective shift into the role of answerer, by dismissing her question and moving on to his claim about all females having bad tempers. In so doing, he re-establishes his dominant discursive position, in a sense restoring the match between his institutional and his discursive roles.

The point about this kind of action, and of looking more closely at how they are accomplished, is that they enable us to gain a more detailed picture of the relationship between speakers' discursive resources, on the one hand, and their institutional status, on the other. If certain kinds of discursive actions can serve as interactional resources for speakers, as I have argued, then theoretically they are available to all participants in any stretch of talk. As we have seen here, A can and does take the opportunity to move into the discursive position of questioner, challenging B in that particular role, and producing some visible unease in the course of the interaction (that is, the long pauses in extract 7.a); the overlapping talk and repair in extract (2.d). However, it is the institutional roles occupied by the participants (the status and number of male police interviewers whose main goal is to interrogate the woman interviewee) that largely determine whether or not the outcome of these actions is successful or not. B has no institutional obligation to participate as an 'answerer', and resists taking up this position when A puts him in it discursively. A, on the other hand, is in the institutional position of having to produce answers to the policemen's questions. If there is any 'disorderly' interaction here then, it seems to originate in an asymmetrical power relationship which gives some participants the right not to respond, while others are under obligation to do so. When a participant is placed discursively in a turn position that in some way conflicts with their institutional role, we can observe a degree of disruption to expected norms of interaction while the police interviewers re-establish their more powerful positions in the talk.

MANAGING CHALLENGES

As we have already seen in relation to the way the woman complainant takes up the position of questioner, being a less powerful participant in terms of your institutional status does not mean that you cannot take up potentially powerful discursive positions in the talk. The woman A does challenge the policemen at several points during the interview, and when challenges of this kind occur, interviewers B and C respond to them in such a way that reinstates them in a more dominant discursive position.

We also saw that on a representational level, the talk is essentially about the reliability of A's version of events, which gets challenged by B and C. The four data extracts below all contain moments in the talk when A takes issue directly with something one or other of the police interviewers has said, either about her behaviour or about her account of the attack.

Extract (8)

```
 1. B:     listen to me (.) I've been sitting here twenty minutes
 2.        half an hour listening to you (.) some of it's the
 3.        biggest lot of bollocks I've ever heard (.) I can get
 4.        very annoyed very shortly (.) one minute you're saying
 5.        it's Coley next minute you're saying it's the
 6.        Meadway=
 7. A: →           =we passed Coley Park
 8. B:     what [happened ]=
 9. C?:         [(happened)]
10. B:                     =I'm sick and tired of the ups and downs
11.        and the ins and outs (.) some of this is better fairytales
12.        than bloody (.) Gretel can do
13.        (2.9)
14. B:     now stop mucking us all about=
15. A: →                      =I'm not mucking you
16.        about=
17. B:        =well I'm not saying to you as you're lying get rid
18.        of the fruitiness get rid of all the beauty about it and
19.        let's get down to [facts and figures]
20. A: →                    [it's not beautiful] at all is it=
21. B:                                            =well
22.        some of it is all this crap about bus stops and (.)
23.        numbers and blue and white tea towels to wipe myself down
24.        with (.) what the hell's gone on if nothing's gone on
25.        let's all pack it off and go home
```

Extract (9)

```
 1. C:     but (.) I'll go as far as to say (.) I think (.)
 2.        you've been a willing party to it (1.4) no seriously
 3.        you're not upset by it you haven't taken a blind bit
 4.        o' notice of anything that's gone on (.) the story
 5.        you've told us (.) is (.) like my colleague says a
 6.        fairy-tale (.) honestly=
 7. A: →                       =well it happened I [(xxx)
 8. B:                                            [well we're
 9.        not saying it didn't happen (.) I'm talking about the
10.        embroidery that goes on (.) around it
```

Extract (10)

```
1. C:     he knows you (.) she left here quite willingly with three
2.        lads
3. A: →   I didn't leave willingly with three lads I didn't even go
4.        with three lads
5. C:     well you left the pub with them
6.        (1.8)
7. A: →   they might've followed me out or (1.0) or something I
8.        don't know
```

Extract (11)

```
1. B:                           [---] all we've got
2.        is your side of the story and you're still making a
```

```
3.          fairytale out of it
4.          (1.0)
5. A: →     I'm not making a fairytale out of it
6.          (1.7)
7. B:       think you are
```

Let us look in some detail now at the talk produced in these sequences, and at what happens when A challenges something contained in a preceding utterance by one or other of the police interviewers. The moments in the talk where this kind of action takes place typically tend to form a three-stage sequence: an interviewer turn which contains some form of evaluation of A's behaviour: 'stop mucking us all about', followed by A's refuting turn 'I'm not mucking you about', and then a third turn in which B or C reaffirm their claim, often in a slightly modified shape, and often starting with the marker 'well'. So we see sequences such as the following:

Extract (8.a)

```
14. B:      now stop mucking us all about=
15. A:                              =I'm not mucking you
16.         about
17. B: →    =well I'm not saying to you as you're lying
```

Extract (8.b)

```
18. B:      get rid of all the beauty about it and
19.         let's get down to [facts and figures ]
20. A:                         [it's not beautiful] at all is it=
21. B: →                                                    =well
22.         some of it is
```

Extract (10.a)

```
1. C:             [---] she left here quite willingly with three
2.         lads
3. A:      I didn't leave willingly with three lads I didn't even go
4.         with three lads
5. C: →    well you left the pub with them
```

In each of the three extracts above, the interviewers use the marker 'well' at the beginning of their third turn. Sacks (1995) has described the use of 'well' in argument sequences as an appositional tying technique, which signals that what is coming next will be a disagreement. Significantly, in this case, it can also signal that in spite of an intervening utterance (for example, A's challenges here) the speaker has not changed their mind about the subject under discussion and that the other person's argument has failed. In the first interviewer turn in the above sequences, there is some kind of assessment either of A's actions or of her account, which A then refutes. In their next turns, the interviewers respond with an utterance prefaced by 'well'. In designing their next turns in this way B and C both acknowledge A's prior refutations, while continuing to question the reliability of her story by signalling that they have not changed their position as a result of them: 'well I'm not saying to you as you're lying', 'well some of it is', 'well you left the pub with them'. The use of 'well' in these sequences functions as another powerful discursive resource through which the police interviewers display their dominant position in the talk by maintaining their version of events as unchanged despite A's arguments.

So, although she does at various points challenge the interviewers' statements, interactionally A is not in a position to get very far with these challenges. She disputes their claims, but they make it clear that they are still holding to their view that she has not been raped. When she designs her utterance in the same way as B and C have been doing, as can be seen in extract (9.a) below, the response from B in the next turn is another countering 'well':

Extract (9.a)

```
 5. C:                    [---] like my colleague says a
 6.       fairy-tale (.) honestly=
 7. A: →                      =well it happened I [(xxx)
 8. B:                                            [well we're
 9.       not saying it didn't happen (.)I'm talking about the
10.       embroidery that goes on (.) around it
```

In line 7, it sounds as though A is about to continue her opposition to interviewer C's evaluation of her account as a 'fairytale', but she is interrupted by B before she is able to get very far with her turn. B's interrupting utterance is produced using exactly the same turn-initial 'well' format, enabling him to continue to build his scepticism about her story, 'the embroidery that goes on around it', and prevent her from moving into a stronger discursive position at that moment.

To summarise the points I have been making here, we have seen that, although she is clearly in a less powerful position than the police interviewers, the woman complainant is able to take up a number of potentially more powerful discursive positions in the talk. At several points she challenges the policemen's construction of her as a willing participant in the events she describes, and one way that she does this is by directly refuting statements that they make about her. The policemen's most frequent response to these refutations is to use turn-initial 'well' utterances, which enables them to acknowledge A's challenge while continuing to build up their own version of her story, so these challenges do not produce any lasting changes in the discursive positions occupied by the participants. Where she is more successful at shifting discourse roles is when she manages to take up the position of questioner. As we have seen in extracts (7.a) and (2.d) above, this creates a discursive 'obligation' to provide an answer which the interviewers have to work harder at avoiding.

CONCLUSIONS

I have argued in this chapter that we cannot account for power in talk simply by mapping discourse roles on to institutional roles. What we need to look at in more detail is precisely how the institutional participant roles occupied by speakers can construct asymmetrical rights and obligations in terms of the discursive actions they can take, and how speakers deal with those occasions in the talk when they are positioned interactionally in a role that in some way conflicts with their institutional relationship.

In the context of this police interview data, it seems to be the case that certain turn positions afford the possibility of more powerful discursive actions than others. The third-turn position in a three part sequence, such as question, response and receipt, or statement, refutation and continuer, is typically occupied by the police interviewers, and from that position they are better able to control the direction of the talk in terms of selecting topics and building arguments. So when A manages to design her challenge in the form of a question, she moves temporarily into a more powerful position as she has potential access to that third-turn position. This may be one reason why the police interviewers do more discursive work to resist the role of answerers.

However, although the question of control in talk can be conceived of partly as a matter of managing to take up certain types of turn, from which you may be able to constrain the actions of the speaker taking up the next one, this does not seem to be the whole story. In the police interview, B and C are able to resist this positioning and are able to do things like change topic rather than answer a question. This would suggest that they reserve the right to occupy the position of questioner but refuse to occupy that of answerer. In other words, when A is in the position of questioner, there is no obligation on B and C to provide an answer.

Another factor which contributes to the power relations between participants is the type of discursive practices which shape the ideological coherence of the talk. This is particularly evident here in the language the policemen use in their descriptions of the complainant's story. By taking up an evaluatory position in relation to A's complaint, the interviewers B, C and D are the more powerful 'categorisers' in the talk, assessing A's account of the attack as 'crap about bus stops', 'lot of bollocks' and 'better fairytales than bloody Gretel can do'. Once her story has been recast in this way, A does not construct any alternative categories to describe what happened to her. Her account (in which at various points she has in fact given a large amount of detail, facts and figures, including the amount of a bus fare, a description of the room she was taken to, etc.) is always subject to the interviewers' assessments, and once these assessments are in play her main line of challenging them is through denials: 'I'm not mucking you about', 'I'm not making a fairytale out of it' rather than through alternative representations of the events. Control of the talk, then, also seems to be a matter of whose particular terms of representation get to be the dominant categories. In this case, regardless of whatever the 'facts' of the case might have been, the discursive practices displayed in the coherence of the policemen's talk produce a trivialisation of rape, and of women's reactions to it, by a process of insult and ridicule.

I have described this interview as inherently asymmetrical on three counts: (1) in terms of gender, (2) in terms of the number of participants in each role and (3) in terms of the relative institutional and social status that holds in this encounter. These three asymmetries translate into unequal distribution of discursive power in very real terms. B and C not only reserve the right *not* to take up certain positions in the talk, they can also take discursive actions that A cannot, such as making threats and accusations and producing aggravated directives: 'I can get very annoyed very shortly', 'listen to me', 'now stop mucking us all about'. The institutional status of the police interviewers in relation to A results in their being able to make more effective use of a range of interactional resources than she is. B and C are in a position to threaten, accuse and make assessments, whereas A is in the position of having to deal with those actions. One of the principal means of exercising power discursively is through institutionally grounded rights to take certain actions in the talk, and, in unequal status encounters, those rights are not held equally by all participants. One might speculate that if the woman interviewee had engaged in the same kind of actions as the police interviewers, in view of her past history of depression and mental health problems, she would probably only have succeeded in reinforcing her already relatively powerless position.

Finally, I have argued that orderly discourse, in terms of the interactive structure of talk, is not necessarily a product of shared or 'naturalised' commonsense assumptions, as has previously been suggested. Rather, I have tried to show how institutionally inscribed relations of power and status do not determine the actions that are possible for speakers to take, but do affect the outcomes of those actions in the ensuing talk. I have also suggested that institutional status can privilege certain discursive practices over others. At the level of representation and ideological coherence, these practices secure the overall intelligibility and coherence of a participant's utterances within and across turns, but not necessarily the coherence of all the participants throughout the talk. In this particular case, the police construction of A's account as unreliable because of her previous mental history, and their commonsense assumptions about appropriate resistance to rape, are the dominant discourses mobilising the interviewers' statements, but not those of the woman complainant. Orderly discourse, then, is an interactive phenomenon that is produced between individual participants in the talk, rather than the product of an ideologically coherent structure shared by all participants.

The data I have chosen to analyse here were taken from talk in an institutional context where the asymmetries were particularly marked. Through this analysis, I have been able to make some quite specific claims about what discursive power might be, where it is observable and what participants can do with it as an interactive resource. In the chapters that follow, I will be dealing with examples of talk from other contexts where these asymmetries are not so marked, to see whether powerful discursive positions are maintained in similar ways, through restricted access and effectiveness of discursive resources and through institutionally differentiated rights and obligations for speakers.

NOTES

1. This is drawn from frame and script theory in cognitive science (Minsky, 1985; Schank and Abelson, 1977) which has been used to describe structures of knowledge about the world in pragmatic theories of interpretation within CDA (for example, Van Dijk, 1985, 1998).

2. Stuart Hall has described naturalised ideologies as 'the politics of signification', that is, 'the means by which collective socical understandings are created – and thus the means by which consent for particular outcomes can be effectively mobilised' (1982: 70).

3. This programme was made in 1980 for a TV documentary series 'Police'. The data used here have appeared in various places in different forms (for example, Thornborrow, 1991; Scannell, 1996). Both the transcript and the analysis have been substantially revised for this chapter.

4. At one stage in the tribunal the defendant actually makes the point that the complainant was not behaving in a way he understood as resistance: 'I don't understand the logic of . . . no I'm sorry. I do not think it's appropriate to get back into bed with somebody who you claim was taking advantage of you' (Ehrlich, 1998: 153).

4

QUESTIONS
AND CONTROL:
MANAGING TALK IN
A RADIO PHONE-IN

In many institutional contexts for talk, the role of questioner is considered to be a more powerful interactional position than the role of answerer. In chapter 3, we saw that in the context of a police interview, questioning is a discursive resource that can produce different interactional outcomes when used by participants who have different institutional identities and unequal institutional status. In this chapter I turn to the role of questioner in a rather different context, talk in calls to a radio phone- in programme.[1] In radio phone-in programmes, it is generally acknowledged that the programme host who takes the calls is in an interactionally stronger position than the caller (Barnard, 2000). But how does this actually come about? By focusing on one specific programme as an illustration, through an analysis of the organisation of the calls, particularly the opening sequences, question formats and call endings, I show how the potentially powerful speaker role of questioner is interactionally 'defused' through the participatory framework of the talk. I will argue that the mediated interactional structure of calls to this programme constrains the range of possible actions available to callers in their institutional position as questioners, so that, in the organisation of talk in this phone-in, callers are positioned in such a way that their potentially powerful discursive role as questioner is attenuated.

QUESTIONS AS POWERFUL DISCURSIVE ACTIONS

The function of questions as a potentially powerful resource in talk has been central to the study of institutional discourse, particularly where those participants who are doing the questioning also have institutionally inscribed identities which affect the asymmetrical distribution of speaker rights and obligations in the talk, as we saw in the previous chapter. Harvey Sacks (1995) observed that in conversation, 'a person who asks a question has a right to talk again afterwards' (Vol. I: 49) and that 'as long as one is in the position of doing the questions, then in part one has control of the conversation' (Vol. I: 55). Conversely, being in the role of answerer can limit the possibilities available to speakers. In an analysis of courtroom interaction, Paul Drew noted that usually 'anyone in the position of answering is restricted to dealing with just what's in the prior question' (1992: 506). Indeed, in courtroom settings, police interviews and medical examinations, as well as in many other forms of institutional interaction, the role of questioner is typically occupied by a participant whose institutional status is such that that the range of actions they can take is generally much broader than the participant who is in the role of answerer. As a result, this puts them in a much stronger interactional position to influence and direct the talk. The radio phone-in programme, on the other hand, is a context for talk where the relationships between participants are such that the interactional status of the people 'doing the questions' is not accompanied by a correspondingly powerful institutional status.

The data presented here are taken from a series of phone-ins broadcast by the BBC radio station 'Radio One' in June 1987, just prior to the general election in that year.[2] In these programmes, listeners were invited to call in on three consecutive days to the leaders of the three main political parties of the day (the incumbent prime minister, Margaret Thatcher, Neil Kinnock, the leader of the Labour Party, and David Steel, one of the leaders of the Liberal-Democrat 'Alliance'), with questions about policy. The programme I analyse here dealt particularly with issues of concern to young people, including questions about unemployment, youth training schemes, student loans and housing. One of the callers was as young as twelve. The phone-in host was Simon Bates, and the studio guest was Margaret Thatcher. The programme featured over twenty calls from listeners throughout England and Wales. (In the transcripts, the names of all callers have been changed.)

A radio phone-in programme provides an opportunity for lay participation in media discourse (cf. Livingstone and Lunt, 1994), and, in this particular programme, an occasion for some direct contact between a high profile political figure (here, the prime minister) and ordinary members of the public. This contact is established through the mediating role of the host, who introduces callers, often ends the calls and sometimes intervenes in the exchanges between the callers and the guest politician. Occasionally, the host also addresses a question to the guest, Margaret Thatcher. The basic interactional format these calls follow consists of an opening greetings sequence, followed by a question/answer sequence, where the caller asks a question and the guest provides a response in what is typically an extended turn at talk. This type of extended answer has been analysed in the context of news interviews, where the interviewee typically gets a longer answer turn than in an ordinary conversational context (cf. Greatbach, 1988; Harris, 1991; Heritage and Greatbach, 1991). In some calls there is an offer of a second or 'supplementary' question slot to the caller, in others the host asks a follow-up question before ending the call and moving on to the next caller.

STRUCTURAL ORGANISATION OF THE CALLS

The actions of the host in his role of programme manager, bringing callers online, determining the length of time and number of times they get to talk, organising the transition from one caller to the next and mediating the interaction between the guest and callers, provide a recognisable, structured framework for the talk. But this structure also results in a highly delimited set of possibilities for participation in terms of who gets to do what in the space of a call. As is normally the case in such programmes, the process of selecting the callers and establishing the order of their calls has already taken place off the air, as we can see by the host's comments in the following extracts:

EC 7//03/06/87

```
SB: we may come back to that later on (.) thank you for your call Ian
```

EC 14//03/06/87

```
SB: well hold on [a second]
MT:             [look    ]
SB: Mukbinda because I'd like to bring back (.) if someone else from
    Cardiff in Wales on that (.h) Simon J- actually prime minister I
    think has a a que- complementary question=
MT:                                          =mmhm=
SB:                                               =about unemployment
```

In these two examples, the host is clearly referring to an already pre-determined order of calls and topics, where callers have already been allocated a particular topic slot in the programme. Since calls from listeners are initially received off the air, the openings of the calls as they are broadcast bear little resemblance to the openings of the kind of telephone calls described by Emmanuel Schegloff (1972, 1979) and this has particular consequences for participants in terms of the types of turn available to them, as we shall see.

Although talk within the context of a popular national radio station may appear less formal than in some other institutional settings, the organisation of the talk in this phone-in nevertheless exhibits a number of the structural regularities and constraints typically found in institutional interaction, in terms of the number of pre-allocated turns and the distribution of turn types between speakers (Drew and Heritage, 1992). In particular, the opening sequences of the calls, and their three-party participatory framework, construct an asymmetrical context for talk in which the potentially powerful interactional role of caller as questioner is attenuated by the structural possibilities open to them; in other words, the type of turns they can take as the call progresses through its various stages. Let us look now at the first of these stages, the call opening.

CALL OPENING SEQUENCES

In most calls to this phone-in programme, callers do not come on air and ask their question straight away. Some quite complex interactional work usually has to take place before callers are in a position to ask a question and, even when they are in that position, several things can happen before they get round to asking it. The first issue that has to be dealt with by all participants is the three-party structure of the talk; the second is that two of the participants share the same studio space, while the other is a non-co-present participant who only shares air space. So the business of bringing all the speakers into the participatory framework has to be accomplished before any further talk can take place, and this is what takes up the opening moments of the call.

The openings of most calls to a radio phone-in follow a fairly routine pattern. This pattern typically consists of a three- or four-turn sequence in which each participant takes at least one turn as in the following call:

EC 5//03/06/87

```
SB:      it's 01580 double 4 double 1 you're on line to the
         prime minister and we'll go to Derek J- in
         Portsmouth in Hampshire. hello Derek
Caller: hello.
MT:      hello Derek
Caller: hello.
```

Here, we can see a four-part greetings exchange first between host and caller, then between guest and caller. In the next example, the host supplies an 'online' cue but no greeting component, and the greetings exchange takes place between guest and caller:

EC 9//03/06/87

```
SB:      → [---] from Kevin J- in Coventry in the west midlands
         you're on line to the prime minister.
MT:      hello Kevin=
Caller:           =erm hello Mrs Thatcher.
```

Here, in a three-part exchange, Kevin is brought online by the host, and then greeted by MT. In calls which diverge from this pattern, usually some problem has occurred that needs dealing with, often to do with clarifying callers' names. As we can see in the two examples above, the host, in his role as manager of the talk, always takes the first turn in the sequence, and begins by identifying the caller by name and also by their geographical location (there was only one call in the data where the caller was not geographically located in the host's opening turn). This first host turn can contain up to three components: a caller identification, a greetings token, and an online cue. The identification usually comes first, but as we shall see variations occur in the ordering of the other two components, which can affect what happens in the next turn. Typical examples of the host's call opening utterances are:

EC 2//03/06/87

```
SB: [---] Sophie P- (.) in Sudbury in Suffolk (.)good
    evening you're on line to the prime minister.
```

EC 16//03/06/87

```
SB: [---] Shan C- from Maidstone in Kent hello you're
    on line to the prime minister
```

The function of the host's first turn is ostensibly to bring the caller into the participatory frame by identifying them (out of a set of possible next callers) by name and location, and to open what Levinson (1988) has termed a 'channel link' to the third party by giving the cue 'you're on line' to callers. This opening turn puts the caller in a rather different position from callers in ordinary telephone call openings. Schegloff (1972) has described the opening sequence of a telephone call as a set of adjacency pairs,[3] as follows:

```
Caller:    {summons
Receiver:  {response
Caller:    {greetings (1) (+ identification)}
Receiver:  {greetings (2)                    }
Caller:    first topic slot
```

After the 'summons' of the telephone ring, the call receiver speaks first, and the caller speaks next and usually also provides the first topic of the call. So in Schegloff's model, after the initial summons/response adjacency pair, it is the caller who initiates the greeting sequence and who gets to give the reason for their call in the first topic slot. In the on-air opening of a call to the radio phone-in, the order of the sequence which could be compared to a summons/response type pair is reversed in so far as the host could be seen to 'summon' the caller in his first turn, and the caller to respond to this summons in the next. We can see this pattern in the following extracts:

EC 18//03/06/87

```
SB:        Sally A- from Newham in London hello.
Caller: →  yes hello.
```

EC 8//03/06/87

```
SB:        Ivan W- you're on line to the prime minister in
           Aylesbury in Bucks.
Caller: →  yeah hello er Mrs Thatcher
```

Both these callers respond with a turn-initial 'yes'. One interpretation of the occurrence of this 'yes' here is that it functions as a response to the host's summoning action in the prior turn, where he identifies the next caller in line to come on air (although there are differing accounts of this 'yes' that I will discuss later in the chapter). According to Schegloff's model of telephone call openings, the call initiator is the person in the position of doing the summoning, the greeting and the first topic selection, while the call receiver is the person being called upon to speak. In the two opening turns of the phone-in call these positions are reversed, since the host speaks first and the caller speaks next, thus shifting the relationship between participants in the call from the one which holds in ordinary telephone call openings described above. We therefore can show the order of speaker turns in the opening sequence of the radio phone-in call as follows:

```
Host:    summons + online cue [+ greeting]
Caller:  response [+ greeting]
```

Furthermore, in Schegloff's model, the sequential 'rules'[4] of the summons/answering sequence put the call receiver in the position of having to listen to the caller, whereas in these phone-in call openings that obligation is incumbent on the caller, who is in the position of responding to the host's initial identification and greeting. Again, the opening sequences of these calls differ from ordinary phone calls, since they put the caller into the position of responding to the host rather than the other way round.

GREETINGS SEQUENCES

Although in the two extracts above both callers respond to the host's first turn with a turn-initial 'yes', which I have described as a response token to a prior summons, this is not typical of calls in the corpus. Out of a corpus of twenty call openings, only two callers began their turns this way; in most other cases, callers start with a greeting in their first turn, as illustrated in the following extracts:

EC 3//03/06/87

```
SB:        [---] Shirley H- from Hailsham in Essek- in Sussex
           I beg your pardon Shirley hi
Caller:  → hello
SB:        you're on line to the prime minister
MT:        hello Shirley
Caller:    Mrs Thatcher [---]
```

EC 5//03/06/87

```
SB:        it's 01580 double 4 double 1 you're on line to the
           prime minister and we'll go to Derek J- in
           Portsmouth in Hampshire. hello Derek
Caller:  → hello.
MT:        hello Derek
Caller:  → hello. [---]
```

EC 7//03/06/87

```
SB:      Ian C- from Ilfracombe in Devon welcome
Caller:  hello
```

In these three calls, the greetings component of the host's opening turn occurs in turn-final position, after the caller identification. The interactional effect that this has is to bring callers into the participatory framework of the call through a greetings adjacency sequence in which the host provides the first 'pair-part', and the caller supplies the second. So the first type of turn, that callers get to take up, positions them interactionally as the 'person greeted', rather than greetings initiator as would be the case in Schegloff's model above. Once again, the consequence of this is to reverse the role relationship of call initiator and call receiver which holds in other telephone calls:

```
Receiver (host): greetings (1)
Caller:          greetings (2)
```

rather than

```
Caller:   greetings (1)
Receiver: greetings (2)
```

A further feature of these openings is that, since there are three participants in the call, some form of contact between the caller and guest needs to be established. Callers generally do not go straight from a greeting in their first turn to a question without some prior contact with the person to whom they are going to ask that question (although see call 1 below which I discuss later as an exception to this pattern). Before callers get to the main point of their call, which is the business of asking a question, the participation framework has to be extended to include the guest. This happens in three different ways in the calls to this phone-in: either the guest takes the second turn in the sequence, and the caller takes third turn, as in the following call:

EC 9//03/06/87

```
SB:       [---] from Kevin J- in Coventry in the west midlands
          you're on line to the prime minister.
MT:       hello Kevin=
Caller:              =erm hello Mrs Thatcher.
```

or there is a further two-turn exchange between the caller and guest after the host/caller greeting sequence:

EC 18//03/06/87

```
SB:     Sally A- from Newham in London hello.
Caller: yes hello.
MT:     hello Sally.
Caller: hello.
```

The third variation happens when the caller uses a 'pivotal' turn and greets the guest directly:

EC 6//03/06/87

```
SB:     OK Roger F- in Runcorn in Cheshire you're on line
        to the prime minister.
Caller: hello (.) Mrs Thatcher.
MT:     [hello]
Caller: [erm  ]
```

EC 10//03/06/87

```
SB:      Malcolm P- in Clifton in Bristol hello.
Caller: hello. [good evening ]Mrs Thatcher
MT:              [hello Malcolm]
Caller: erm [---]
```

In call 6, where there is no host greeting, the caller greets the guest directly, while in call 10 the caller does a double greeting, first in response to the host, then addressed to the guest. In these two calls, having greeted MT, Roger and Malcolm are ready to move straight into their questions without waiting for a second greeting pair part from MT, as can be seen from the overlap that occurs in both openings.

As I noted earlier, the only call where the caller does move directly into asking a question without engaging in an initial greetings sequence is the very first one in the phone-in. However, in the preceding talk the host had introduced the guest and a greetings exchange had already taken place between the two just prior to the host's first call opening turn. Here is the first call:

EC 1//03/06/87

```
1. SB:      [---] tonight I'm joined by the prime minister Mrs
2.          Thatcher (.) good evening
3. MT:      good evening
4. SB:      thank you for coming and lets get straight to the
5.          calls Keith M- (.) from Barnstaple in North Devon
6.          good evening
7. Caller: hello yes uh my question uh to the prime minister
8.          is on health
```

The occurrence of an immediately prior completed greetings sequence (lines 2 and 3) may explain this first caller's move from a greeting to a question within his first turn, since the guest has already in effect been brought into the participatory frame by the host.

The longest call opening of all in the corpus extended over six turns which included a greetings exchange between host and caller, followed by an online cue overlapping with a guest greeting (lines 3 and 4), then a further full greetings exchange between caller and guest:

EC 12//03/06/87

```
1. SB:      Susan H- in Cheltenham in Gloucester hello
2. Caller: hello
3. MT:      [hello Susan   ]
4. SB:      [you're on line] to the prime minister.=
5. Caller:                                  =thank you
6.          hello Mrs Thatcher.
7. MT:      hello Susan
```

Here, the simultaneous production of MT's first greeting and the host's online cue is followed by the caller's acknowledgement 'thank you' (line 5) of the host's overlapped online cue. There then follows a complete greetings sequence (lines 6 and 7) between the caller and MT, who repeats her overlapped greeting turn (line 3) in response to Susan's first part greetings token (line 6). This call opening has been extended by the host's delay of his online cue until the fourth turn in the sequence, until all three participants have been properly brought into the frame. So to some extent the call openings are dependent for their completion on the host's mediating action of bringing callers 'on line'.

In three-party talk, who gets to speak next can be interactionally problematic, and this is particularly the case in mediated three-party talk where one participant is not physically co-present with the other two, and cannot rely on gaze or other non-verbal speaker selection cues. In these calls, when a greeting addressed to the caller occurs at the end of the host's opening turn, then the caller can reasonably expect to take up the next turn as directly addressed next speaker. When the greetings component occurs earlier in the host's turn, or, as in two calls, when it is absent altogether, there are then two potential next speakers. This frequently results in overlapping utterances where caller and guest both self select to take the next turn, as in the calls below:

EC 2//03/06/87

```
SB:      [---] Sophie P- (.) in Sudbury in Suffolk (.)
         good evening you're on line to the prime minister.
Caller: [h'llo
MT:      [hello Sophie
Caller: hello.
```

EC 11//03/06/87

```
SB:       Edward L- you're on line to Mrs Thatcher.
Caller: → [good evening.]
MT:      → [hello Edward] good evening
```

EC 19//03/06/87

```
SB:       [---] Phil D in Kingswood in Bristol hello you're
          on line to the prime minister
Caller: → [hello]
MT:      → [hello] Phil
Caller:   hello.
```

In these calls, where there is an overlap of greetings between guest and caller, the overlapping stretch is repaired, and the greeting token repeated, so that a hearably complete greetings exchange occurs between caller and guest.

From the evidence in these call openings, in general we can see that callers do not ask their question before all participants have been brought into frame, and, usually, not before a completed greetings sequence has taken place between caller and guest. What callers do in their first turn is not just a response to the host's identifying summons, but a response to an interactional move which brings them 'on air' and into the participatory frame within which they will get to ask their question. However, to return to a comparison with the sequencing rules of Schegloff's model, this move positions them as call recipients rather than initiators, as summoned rather than summoners, and often as the speaker taking second greetings turn rather than first.

GETTING 'ON-LINE'

This opening turn in which the host names and locates the caller is multi-functional. Firstly, as we have seen, it is the host's signal, or summons, to the caller that it is their turn in the scheduled sequence of calls to go on air, and, as I have also noted, some callers respond to this identification by saying 'yes' in their next turn, as a response to the host's summons:

EC 1//03/06/87

```
SB:        thank you for coming and let's get straight to the
           calls Keith M- (.) from Barnstaple in North Devon
           good evening
Caller:  → hello yes uh my question uh to the prime minister
           is on health [---]
```

EC 18//03/06/87

```
SB:        Sally A- from Newham in London hello
Caller:  → yes hello
```

A second function is to name the caller for the wider constituency of programme listeners, and a third, related function, is to identify the caller for the purposes of the guest who can then use the caller's name in a following greeting sequence. Name checks can also occur in the opening sequences between caller and guest as in the following extracts:

EC 6//03/06/87

```
SB:      OK Roger F- in Runcorn in Cheshire you're on line
         to the prime minister.
Caller: hello (.) Mrs Thatcher.
MT:      [hello]
Caller: [erm= ]
MT:               =that was Roger was it=
SB:                              =Roger [yes it was
Caller:                                 [it is yeah
```

EC 13//03/06/87

```
SB:      thank you very much indeed Susan uh Mukbinda B=
MT:                                                 =oh my
         [goodness            so      ]=
SB:      [that's Mukbinda from Birmingham]
MT:      =how do we pronounce you Mukb-=
Caller:                              =it's Mukbinda
MT:      Mukbinda right we've got it
```

With the exception of these calls, where establishing caller identity becomes prob-lematic,[5] if the signal 'you're online' is not present in the host's opening turn, callers do not usually go ahead with their question until it has been supplied. The following calls show this in practice:

EC 12//03/06/87

```
SB:     Susan H- in Cheltenham in Gloucester hello
Caller: hello
MT:     hello Susan
SB:     you're on line to the prime minister
Caller: I'd just like to ask [---]
```

EC 3//03/06/87

```
SB:     thank you very much indeed for your call Sophie
        Shirley H- from Hailsham in Essek- in Sussex I
        beg your pardon Shirley hi
Caller: hello
SB:     you're on line to the prime minister
MT:     hello Shirley
Caller: Mrs Thatcher (.) I'd like to know um [---]
```

EC 7//03/06/87

```
SB:     Ian C- from Ilfracombe in Devon welcome
Caller: hello
MT:     [hello ]
SB:     [what's] your question please
```

EC 19//03/06/87

```
SB:     Shelley L- in Hackney in London hello Shelley
Caller: hello
MT:     Shelley
Caller: hello
MT:     hello [dear go ahead  ]
Caller:       [(I'd just) like] to ask you [---]
```

The only exception to this pattern was call 10, where the caller proceeds with his question turn without being given an online signal by the host:

EC 10//03/06/87

```
SB:     Malcolm P- in Clifton in Bristol hello
Caller: hello [good evening ] Mrs Thatcher
MT:           [hello Malcolm]
Caller: erm (.) if the Tories were be to be returned to a
        third term in office (.) what would be the home-
        what would the homeless have to look forward to (.) [any]
(MT):   [.hh]
Caller: can I continue sorry
MT:     (continue)
```

So, although it is perfectly possible for callers to move into their question turn without the host first providing a channel opening cue, as we can see here in call 10, in general callers did not do so. Even when they have already engaged in a greetings sequence with the guest, and it is open to them to continue without some form of 'online' cue from the host, the majority of callers wait for it to be produced before taking their question turn. This claim seems further warranted if we consider that, although overlap does sometimes occur between caller and guest in greetings sequences, there is no instance of overlapping speech between a host online cue and the onset of a caller question turn in any of the calls.

Now, to sum up so far, the organisation of call openings in this context can be shown to have two main consequences in terms of how callers are positioned in relation to the host and guest. Firstly, the summoner/summoned relationship in ordinary telephone call openings between caller and receiver is reversed in the phone-in, thereby shifting the obligation to listen away from the host and on to the caller. Secondly, if the 'on-line' cue is absent or delayed, the tendency of callers to wait until it has been produced before going ahead with their question suggests that this cue functions not just as a channel opener, but as a host signal to callers to move into taking their question turn. In other words, the right of access to a caller's question turn is perceived as available through the host's mediation, rather than being directly accessible to the caller once the business of establishing three-party participation through a greetings sequence has taken place. As a result of these structural relationships, the potentially powerful role of caller as questioner is partially mitigated through the institutional constraints which come into play during the opening stages of a call. Through his actions of caller identification and channel opening, the host is setting up an interactional environment which places callers in a subordinate position from a discursive point of view before they get to take up their question turns.

DOING THE QUESTIONS

In many other contexts for telephone call openings, it is the caller who has the interactional job of getting to the point of the call, that is, to the 'first topic' position. After the initial greetings sequences, a caller will usually give the reason for their call (as we saw earlier on page 64). In the openings of calls to this phone-in, callers have to move from a position where they are being brought 'on air' into the participatory framework of the call, to a position where they can ask their question, which is the main point of the call. So here, not only are callers shifted out of their role as call initiators, as described above, they are also shifted out of their role as 'first topic' initiators, as the reason and substance of their call is already known to the other participants, since the order of calls and topics is established before going on air. What frequently happens is that before they get to the question as such, most callers produce a framing utterance which repositions them as having a question to ask. Examples of these framing devices can be seen in the following extracts:

EC 12//03/06/87

Caller: I'd just like to ask [---]

EC 17//03/06/87

```
Caller: hello. I'd like to ask erm [---]
```

EC 1//03/06/87

```
Caller: hello yes uh my question uh to the prime minister
        is on health [---]
```

EC 3//03/06/87

```
Caller: Mrs Thatcher (.) I'd like to know um if you come to power
```

EC 9//03/06/87

```
Caller: thank you. erm (.) first of all I'd just really (.)
        like to ask about the small businesses [erm]
```

These framing utterances seem to function as a transitional device to get from one kind of action to another, in other words, between the business of getting on line to the business of asking their question, and the fact that most callers design their question turns in this way seems to indicate their reorientation at that moment to the role of questioner.

Another frequently occurring feature in callers' question turns is the presence of an utterance such as 'yes uh' or 'erm' or 'er', which also functions as a transitional device between moving out of a greetings exchange and moving into asking a question. In an analysis of the opening sequences in calls to talk radio, Ian Hutchby (1999) has argued that these opening exchanges 'provide a space in which participants can align themselves in terms of given speaker identities (those of caller and host) and move into the specific topical agenda of the call' (p. 47). The routine production of what Hutchby terms 'buffer' devices (such as 'erm', short intakes of breath, and short pauses) in call openings is described as part of a micro-process whereby participants work through a series of footings from 'speaker-in-waiting' to a position of 'full speakership' (p. 53). Specifically, this is a process through which the caller can take up the role of a topic initiator, as illustrated in the call below:

H: 23.1.89:2.1

```
Host:   Pete is calling from Ilford. Good morning.
Caller: .h Good morning Brian. (0.4) .hh What I'm
        phoning up is about the cricket ...
```

(Hutchby, 1999: 46)

There are some clear similarities between the format of this call opening and the openings of the Radio One phone-in, particularly in the design of call 1 below:

EC 1//03/06/87

```
SB:         thank you for coming and let's get straight to the calls
            Keith M- (.) from Barnstaple in North Devon good evening
Caller: →   hello yes uh my question uh to the prime minister is on
            health (.hh) I'm a nurse [---]
```

Here we can see the caller moving through the same shifts in footing in his first turn from initial engagement with the host in a greetings sequence, through a buffer device 'yes uh', to take up a position of full speakership. However, this does not capture the whole picture. One first difference arises because of the fact that topic initiation is not on the agenda for these callers, since their topic is already substantially 'given' to the other participants in the call. In calls to this phone-in, what callers have to do once the opening sequence is complete is to realign themselves as questioners, and this realignment seems to be the main function of the framing devices they routinely use to preface the production of the question itself. The second difference is that a small but significant number of callers do not produce any question framing or 'buffer' device, and, when this happens, their questions are noticeably different in design from those callers who do produce them, as we will now see. The following extracts exemplify some of the various ways that callers design their question turns in this phone-in:

EC 12//03/06/87

```
Caller: I'd just like to ask you why your government [---]
```

EC 16//03/06/87

```
Caller: um I would like to ask the prime minister on the
        question of first time voters apparently [---]
```

EC 18//03/06/87

```
Caller: hello. I'd like to ask erm if er there's someone who is
        unemployed (.) and under twenty five (.hh) who refuses [---]
```

The question-framing device is present in all these calls, but, while call 16 contains all three elements, call 12 has no buffer device, and, in call 18, the 'erm' occurs after the question frame rather than prior to it.

The caller's question in call 17 below takes a very different form, as he uses grammatically complex and complete clause structures, and the pauses occur at neat syntactic boundaries:

EC 17//03/06/87

```
Caller: =(Mrs) Thatcher. in view of yesterday's party election
        broadcast (.) I would ask you (.) if you think that the
        manner in which you pushed you to the forefront (.) rather
        than your policies (.) leaves you open to personal attack
```

As a result, this question is marked by a much greater level of formality than many of the other questions examined so far. So, while some callers may move through these interactional stages, from greetings sequence and question frame to the production of the question itself, this is by no means always the case. The question in call 17 is more formally structured than many of the others, which probably indicates that the caller had to some extent prepared what they were going to say.

In the next two calls, we can again see that the questions are more formally structured and that these callers seem to be using a rather different register from some of the others:

EC 5//03/06/87

```
Caller: does the prime minister think that in the current employment
        situation (.) where a university degree is no longer a
        guarantee of a job (.) that the conservative's intended (.)
        student loan scheme (.) is justified.
```

EC 7//03/06/87

```
Caller: over the election period prime minister (.) you have been
        accused of not caring (.) something which you have denied (.)
        but how can you claim to care (.) especially (when young) are
        concerned (.) when your government has abolished wages
        councils for under twenty ones [---]
```

The marked increase in the level of formality of these question is particularly noticeable in call 7, where the caller engages in an extended question turn, which from its grammatical structure as well as its intonation contours has clearly either been well rehearsed or is being read out by the caller. In call 5 the caller uses a third term address form 'does the prime minister think' while call 3 is relatively informal: 'Mrs Thatcher I'd like to know'. The slight pause which occurs between 'Mrs Thatcher' and 'I'd like to know' could be read as a transitional shift of footing, but it does not sound like one. The caller's use of 'Mrs Thatcher' here is as a direct address term rather than the final part of a greetings sequence, and it does not finish on a falling tone, as is the case for other end-of-greetings sequences.

What marks out the difference between these calls and others in the phone-in is the absence of question-framing devices, such as 'I'd like to know . . .'. This framing device, which occurs in all but the most formal question formats, can take different forms (underlined in the following examples):

EC 1//03/06/87

```
Caller: hello yes uh my question uh to the prime minister is on
        health (. hh) I'm a nurse in (.) a London teaching hospital
        and (.) my question is this [---]
```

EC 4//03/06/87

```
Caller: that's right (.h)er (mine's) a bit of a light weight
        question this er I just wondered er Mr Kinnock has er
        recorded a video (.) er with Tracy Ullmann er David Steel
        has [er       app]eared=
SB:         [((laughs))]
Caller: =in one as well I wondered if y-you'd chance to let down
        your hair whether or not you'd appear in a video?
```

In call 1, we find a double frame: 'my question uh to the prime minister is on health' and 'my question is this', while in call 4, the framing takes up most of this caller's question turn as he uses a similar structure: '(mine's) a bit of a light weight question this' and two additional frames: 'I just wondered', to draw attention to the non-serious nature of the question.

Callers sometimes also preface what they have to ask by giving some contextualising information, which functions to situate their question within a more personal frame:[6]

EC 6//03/06/87

```
Caller: er I work for a local building society (.) and in order to
        get promotion (.) er I need to move down south (.) now my
        concern is this (differing) in house prices (.) up here (.)
        down there (.) er I understand [---]
```

EC 8//03/06/87

```
Caller: yeah I come from a one parent family (.) a difficult(y) my
        mother has found in finding work (.) is the poverty tr- trap
        (.) where the initial tax paid is (.) too high (.) an'it's
        not (.) you know not worth paying the transport costs
        etcetera (.) just wondering what measures the next
        conservative government would do [(s-) er]
```

EC 15//03/06/87

```
Caller: ok I voted conservative in the last election and I would
        do so again (bar) from the unemployment problem (.) so my
        question is would you be prepared to resign control of the
        government [---]
```

In each of these calls, the additional personalised frame to the question is followed by a question-framing device: 'so my question is', 'just wondering', 'now my concern is this'. From these calls, we can see that the time it takes a caller to make the transition between finishing the greetings exchange and getting to the point when they ask their question can vary considerably. The callers' reorientation to the role of questioner is therefore variably accomplished through their choice of question format and the way they frame their question as well as through their choice of register and mode of address. In this corpus of calls, only four callers do not use a question-framing device such as 'I would ask you' or 'I'd like to know'. One of these was the youngest caller (12 years old) to the programme, who uses direct second-person address:

EC 2//03/06/97

```
Caller: hello. (.h) what are you going to do if you get voted in
        again about people like my dad (.) when they go after jobs
        (.)are told (.) they are too old at forty
```

and the three most formal questions, whose prosodic contour and grammatical structure indicate that they have been carefully prepared, as we saw in calls 5 and 7 and, similarly, in call 11 below:

EC 11//03/06/87

```
Caller: erm your famous quote from St Francis of Assisi in 1979 (.)
        talks of your premiership (.) bringing harmony truth faith
        and hope (.) do you consider you've achieved this.
```

So far then, I have suggested that the way callers design their question turns in this phone-in has to do primarily with the work of repositioning themselves as questioners, and they do this in ways which range from the highly informal, and also heavily framed type of question that I noted in call 4, to the much more formally structured question in call 7. In this call, the caller engages in the kind of question design that is more typically found in political interviews (where interviewers often precede their question with a series of contextualising utterances[7]) before actually producing his question: 'does this not show that your government does not care about the young'.

Secondly, I have shown that when callers move straight from a greetings sequence to their question, without any interactional reorientation to their status as questioners, then this is accompanied by a similar shift in register, from the more informal framed questions, to the formal structure and design of those where framing is absent. So by using greater levels of formality in register and grammatical structure, the three callers in 5, 7 and 11 are designing their question turns in such a way that makes them stand out as noticeably different from most of the other questions. Callers who choose a more formal register for their questions may be using this formality to construct a firmer interactional status for themselves as questioners and, consequently, to construct a more symmetrical framework of interaction with the other more institutionally powerful participants.

THE DESIGN OF HOST QUESTIONS

Callers are not the only questioners in this phone-in; the host also occasionally takes a question turn in a call, usually to follow up some issue related to the caller's first question. The following extracts illustrate some typical host question turns:

EC 2//03/06/87

```
MT:     [---] we'll try to help your father dear as much
        as we can by counselling him and by training him
        for the jobs that are available
SB: →   long term are you optimistic about unemployment
        when people are older
MT:     (.hh) long term yes I am optimistic about unemployment [---]
```

EC 6//03/06/87

```
MT:     [---] they've got to start it up in a place where
        they can keep their costs down (.) from which they
        can sell their goods (.) and from which they can
        get the kind of labour they want to employ
SB:  →  do you recognise the north south divide
```

EC 15//03/06/87

```
MT:     [---] gets an enterprise allowance (.) while he's
        starting up his own business (.) and he gets paid
        forty pounds a week for a year
SB:  →  prime minister some people think that you show lack
        of sympathy for those who are unemployed particularly
        young people (.) ah you sometimes give to some people's
        impression the (.) the idea that they should get up and
        get a job and if they don't then it's their fault is that
        true
```

As can be seen in these extracts, the host moves directly into a question turn without using any of the framing devices produced by callers. The only occasion where the host precedes his question with a framing device is in call 17, and there seems to be strong sequential reasons for this. Here is the host's contribution to this call:

EC 17/a//03/06/87

```
 1. MT: [---] if you put yourself in the front line in politics
 2.      you must expect to be shot at not of course literally
 3.      [but verbally]
 4. SB: [((laughs)) ] are ele[ctions becoming-
 5. MT:                       [so you just don don't don't
 6.      squeal about it it just I don't like it er I don't like
 7.      it if it gets personal because if anyone starts to
 8.      attack you personally (.) and the short answer is well
 9.      you you haven't got any policies then have you
10. SB: er let me be personal and ar- ask you (mm 'n) you've
11.      been accused of [this ] in the papers are elections
12. MT:                  [mmh  ]
13. SB: in this coming- is this country becoming more
14.      presidential
```

First he attempts to take a question turn (line 4) after the possible completion point in the guest's answer (line 3) and, as in the above examples, here there is no transitional device or framing of his question. However, MT has not completed her turn at this point and interrupts him (line 5) to continue with her extended answer, so he fails to get the floor and ask his question. He then tries again (line 10) with a question that in its initial design and structural format is doing the work of positioning him as having a question to ask: 'er let me be personal and ar- ask you' before moving into his institutional role as a 'professional' questioner.

Having misjudged the end of MT's answer to a quite considerable degree, and having been 'talked over' as she finishes her turn, the host seems to have more work to do to reposition himself for a second attempt at his question. He does this by using a transitional 'er', and by framing his question with 'let me be personal and ar- ask you'. The transition between speakers at this point is also strengthened by the host's repeat of MT's use of 'personal', which establishes a clear pivotal link between what has just been said in the preceding turn, and what is going to come up in the next one. The design of the next part of the turn however is a clear move back into establishing his host-as-interviewer role, as he shifts into a more neutral footing (cf. Clayman, 1992) in relation to his question: '(mm 'n) you've been accused of this in the papers [---]'.

From these examples, we can see that the host is clearly constructing a different type of institutionally ratified status through his direct questioning of the guest at any relevant point; his use of a question-framing device is to repair a failed question turn rather than to routinely establish himself in an institutional role as questioner.

FOLLOW-UP TURNS

Having asked their question, which is then responded to by the guest, what do callers do next? Normally, in two-party talk, the person doing the question would get to talk again after an answer of some sort had been supplied. In the context of the phone-in, it is not the caller, but the host, who takes the next turn. In this turn position, he can either invite the caller to come back with a 'supplementary' question, ask one himself, or terminate the call and move on to the next. The following two extracts illustrate the last of these strategies:

EC 1//03/06/87

```
Host: Keith I'm not going to let you come back with a supplementary
      (.) I want to get as many calls in as possible
```

EC 3//03/06/87

```
Host: well that answers that question Neil G in York
      you're on line to Mrs Thatcher
```

In most cases, callers generally wait for the host's invitation to take another turn, which the host phrases as 'coming back':

EC 8//03/06/87

```
Host: would you like to come back Ivan
```

EC 11//03/06/87

```
Host: Edward would you like to come back
```

EC 13//03/06/87

```
Host: Mukbinda would you like to come back
```

EC 18//03/06/87

```
Host:   Sally would you like to come back with a supplementary
```

EC 20//03/06/87

```
Host:   Shelley very quickly come back
```

From this follow-up turn, then, it is possible for the host either to terminate a call or to open up space for further talk by the caller. In effect, when callers do take up a 'supplementary' turn, they do not use it to ask another question, but to comment on some aspect of the 'answer', so in this sense the host's use of the phrase 'come back' is an accurate description of what happens in 'supplementary' caller turns. The host's ability to end a call at this point also puts him, rather than the caller, in the position of judging whether a sufficient answer has been supplied. Once again the potential power of the questioner to respond to a preceding answer is structurally mitigated by the mediating role of the host and by callers' restricted access to the next turn.

In many calls, there is only one question/answer sequence between caller and guest, and for those callers their question turn is the only time they get to speak. In some cases callers are invited to assess the answers they are given:

```
Sophie you're a twelve year old are you happy with the prime
minister's answer

Roger does that answer your question
```

However, if a caller tries to take up a next turn without being invited to do so, then the host intervenes, as in the following call:

EC 5//03/06/87

```
Caller: what (inaudible)
MT:     and sometimes it's thought that they would need more
Host:   hang on one second Derek
MT:     it's a top up loan and not a substitute for a grant
Host:   would you like to come back now
Caller: yes the point I'm trying to make is that [---]
```

The normal pattern seems to be that any subsequent talk by the caller has to be re-initiated via the host, which means that the opportunity for direct interaction between caller and guest is structurally difficult to achieve, although not impossible as we can see in the next extended extract from call 7:

EC 7//03/06/87

```
1. MT:      [---] if you were an employer (.) you couldn't afford
2.          to take young people on (.) at four fifths of the
3.          adult [wage
4. Caller:      [yes but
```

```
 5. MT:      if it was a skilled job (.)(.hh) [and so in our way]
 6. Caller:                                   [(inaudible      )]
 7. MT:      we shall get very many more young people [employed ]
 8. Caller:                                           [you've had]
 9.          eight years to have your say could I have a little (.)
10.          more say please
11. MT:      yes of course
12. Caller:  erm (.) when an employer takes on young people I've
13.          seen (here in) Ilfracombe in the summer (.hh) they
14.          take on adults in in before the high season gets going
15.          (.) once the high season comes (.) they sack the adults
16.          and take on children (.) so it fuels unemployment
17.          and employers just have cheaper labour (.h) you've
18.          talked about students getting wages jobs in the summer (.)
19.          most are under twenty one (.) they have no protection
20.          so what do they do (.) they're forced to take a very
21.          very low wages forced by yourself (.h) before the wages
22.          counc- the wage m- wages weren't all that high (.)
23.          but at least they had some protection (.)
24. MT:      [(.hh)
25. Caller:  you have removed that Mrs Thatcher
26. MT:      [no ]                  [no    ]
27. Host:    [Ian] hang on a [second] I'm going to get the prime
28.          minister [to answer your question
29. MT:               [no I don't accept that
30. Caller:  [you have]
31. MT:      [because ]at that [particular] time there is a [---]
32. Caller:                    [you have ]
```

Here the caller successfully manages to access a non-host-mediated turn, and thereby interact directly with the guest. He makes three attempts to take the floor, overlapping MT's talk (lines 4, 6 and 8), and eventually succeeds in making a direct request for 'a little more say' which MT responds to with 'yes of course' (line 11). Once this caller has managed to talk himself into the position of being able to take another extended follow up turn, it is much more difficult for the host to regain his mediating role, as by this stage (lines 12–29) the other two participants are already engaging in direct interaction without it. When the host does try to intervene (line 27) MT is already responding to the caller, and continues with that response in overlap with the host, while the caller continues to take issue with her (lines 30–2). This is the only instance in the data where a caller manages to do this successfully. At other times, either the host intervenes (as in call 5), which means that the caller relinquishes their attempt to speak again, or the caller's voice is 'faded out' so that MT can talk over the caller, as can be seen at the arrowed sequences in the next extract:

EC 18//03/06/87

```
1. SB:      Sally would you like to come back with a supplementary
2. Caller:  yes I would yes because (.) you haven't really answered
3.          the question as to if if you guarantee a place for
4.          all eighteen twenty five year olds on the job training
5.          scheme (.h) whether erm then they will be not able to
```

```
 6.                benefit like (.) the sixteen to eighteen year olds and
 7.                also (.h) er as far as YTS is concerned (.) er only a
 8.                third of the people who complete YTS (.h) actually get a
 9.                job at the end of it and only twelve per cent of those
10.                people are with erm the same company that they've been
11.                with on the YTS scheme (.hh) and I think that taking
12.                away erm young people's (.h) benefit is little more
13.                than (.) conscription onto er cheap labour schemes
14.         →      the you you just [([---fade out---])]
15. MT:     →                        [it's not conscription at all dear]
16.         →      it's not conscription at all. [no one's forcing you ]
17. Caller: →                                     [(well if (inaudible)]
18. MT:            no one's forcing you to stay at school no one's forcing
19.                you to go to college (.hh) no one is f-forcing you
20.                to go into a job (.) no one is forcing you to go onto
21.                YTS what we're saying is [---]
```

Here, after the host's invitation to 'come back', this caller takes more time to respond and put her point of view. She is interrupted by MT (line 15) and her voice
becomes less audible as MT takes the floor. She then tries to take another turn (line
17) and again is 'faded out' as MT gets to finish her response. While it may be the
case that control of what gets heard in the phone-in lies ultimately with the institutional operator of technical equipment, it seems nevertheless significant to note that
when the host's mediating role breaks down discursively, it can be rectified technically. In other words, when callers manage to occupy discursive roles which reduce
the interactive asymmetry between them and the studio participants, then this is
usually dealt with by resorting to fading out the caller's voice rather than through
spoken intervention by the host.

I have argued here that the turn positions conventionally occupied by host, caller
and guest in the phone-in result in an attenuation of the discursively powerful role
of the caller as questioner. The structural organisation of calls to the programme not
only positions the caller asymmetrically in relation to the other two participants
from a mediated point of view (co-present v. non-co-present speakers) but also constrain the kind of actions it is possible for callers to take, such as taking up third-turn
positions in a question/answer/follow-up sequence. When these constraints are
resisted by callers, as we have seen in the extracts above, then the participation structure, set up in the opening sequence of the call, changes and callers can move into
more powerful discursive positions in the talk.

CALL CLOSINGS

I finish this chapter with a short description of call closings, which are usually
accomplished by the host as swiftly as possible, in order to move on to the next call.
Steven Clayman (1989) has noted that closings in news interviews typically involve
both a reduction and a specialisation of the closing sequences, which hold in more
conversational contexts for talk. There are clearly constraints on time in these

programmes, and, while closings can be quite lengthy matters, in news interviews the need to get the current speaker punctually off air, and the next speaker on, results in shorter closings sequences than in more conversational interaction. In this phone-in data, a typical call closing is accomplished by the host thanking the caller then moving on to directly introduce the next caller:

EC 11//03/06/87

```
Host: Thank you Edward / Suan H- in Cheltenham in Gloucester hello
```

Occasionally, the guest also takes a turn in the closing sequence as in this example:

EC 9//03/06/87

```
Host: Kevin thank you very much for your question
MT:   thank you Kevin
Host: Malcolm P in Clifton in Bristol hello
```

Sometimes there is no 'thank you' sequence addressed to the previous caller, and the host simply moves into getting the next caller on line once MT has reached a turn completion point:

EC 17//03/06/87

```
MT:   and a very good team they are if I may say so (.)
      excellent (.) not bettered anywhere.
Host: Sally A- from Newham in London hello
```

EC 19//03/06/87

```
MT:   more privatisation yes (.) I say (.) governments are not good
      at running business and I think people who can (.) who think
      they can (.) are a little bit arrogant.
Host: Shelley L in Hackney in London hello Shelley
```

The notable absence from most of these call closing sequences is the caller. In only one of the calls does the caller participate in a closing exchange with the guest:

EC 5//03/06/87

```
Host:   Derek come back if you want to one more time
Caller: well thank you for clarifying that issue prime minister
Host:   thank you very much indeed
MT:     thank you very much
```

On this occasion the caller is given an opportunity to respond to the guest by the host: 'come back if you want to'. This caller has been more successful than most in getting access to the floor and pushing his point. Earlier in the call, he had attempted to take a next turn after the guest response to his question, and is the only caller to be invited to take more than one follow-up turn, to 'come back one more time'. This call then is unusual in several respects, in that the caller manages to participate in the interactive framework of the call in a way that many other callers do not. Firstly, he does not frame his question with any transition device, but uses a more formal register with third-person address to 'the prime minister'. Secondly, he tries to take another turn without waiting for host mediation, although the host overrides this action and re-positions him as invited to respond (would you like to come back now) rather than allowing the interaction to proceed between caller and guest. Thirdly, he moves into a question/answer sequence of direct interaction with the guest later in the call:

EC 5//03/06/87

```
Caller: such a loan will stay until they've got a job
MT:     the loan would stay until one gets a job and when
        you do get a job you would expect with a university
        degree that you'd have a very much better paid job
```

Finally, after being offered a further opportunity to speak, he is in a position to initiate the closing sequence of the call. All these factors distinguish this call from most of the others, where the host effectively determines what counts as a sufficient answer from MT before closing the call (as we saw in call 3 above). Call 5 is then unusual in so far as Derek has had more opportunities to put his points across, which may explain why the host specifically brings him into the closing sequence. In most other calls, the host simply moves on to the next call after MT has produced a hearable ending, or marked completion point, in her response turn, illustrated in the next extract:

EC 10//03/06/87

```
MT: well we (.) look we've got a whole programme to do it (.)
    you can put the ball at someone's feet (.) whether they
    kick it or not we don't know but we'll just have to see
```

Callers are rarely in the position to say whether MT's answer is a satisfactory one for them or not, unless they are explicitly invited to do so by the host:

EC 2//03/06/87

```
Host: Sophie are you happy with the prime minister's answer
```

EC 6//03/06/87

```
Host: Roger does that answer your question
```

Possible points of closure in the call are thus managed by the host, who can opt to terminate a call after the completion of a guest response, or to prolong the call either by opening up more space for callers to talk, or by taking a follow-up turn himself:

EC 10//03/06/87

```
Host:  can I just take Malcolm's point
MT:    mm hmm
Host:  I think Malcolm is on about the regulations primarily and the
       difficulties that some young people have [---]
```

To return to a comparison with other contexts for telephone conversations, where the closing sequences are 'a delicate matter both technically, in the sense that they must be so placed that no party is forced to exit while still having compelling things to say, and socially in the sense that both over-hasty and over-slow terminations can carry unwelcome inferences about the social relationships between the participants' (Levinson, 1983: 316), phone-in call closings flout the technical rule, since they are designed to exclude the possibility of callers bringing up other 'compelling things to say' which could cause delays in moving on to the next call. They also flout the social rule in so far as the closing sequence is often hasty in the extreme, particularly towards the end of the programme, when time is running short and there is no closing sequence at all. While in news interviews, Clayman argues that in closing sequences 'interactants co-ordinate their actions to finish "on time" ' (1989: 685), in this phone-in data, callers have little opportunity to participate actively in the closing sequences.

CONCLUSIONS

Through this discussion of calls to a radio phone-in, I have tried to show how the structural organisation and distribution of turn-types, as well as the three-party frame-work for the talk, result in different types of actions being available to different participants. The pre-allocation of different types of turns to some speakers and not others, and particularly the intermediary work of the host, means that callers' access to certain types of interactional positions is constrained, and their potentially power-ful discursive role of questioner is displaced. The call openings bring callers into the talk as 'summoned parties', as call receivers rather than initiators. Callers have to reposition themselves as questioners, and they generally do not take another receipt turn without being explicitly invited to do so by the host. On occasions when callers do succeed in taking up that next receipt turn position, they are then in a much stronger position to interact directly with the guest and gain access to more discurs-ive space in which to make their points. Finally, call closings and, by and large, sufficient answers are determined by the host without caller participation.

Control of the talk in this context is, however, not simply in the hands of the host in his institutional role as mediator; rather, it depends on who gets to occupy part-icular turn positions in the talk. I have argued that the participatory framework of these calls is both asymmetrical, in the sense that not all participants can do the same thing, and constraining, in that access to specific types of turn is restricted to callers. But it is also challenged, as we have seen in some calls, and when callers successfully bring off this challenge the participatory framework changes as caller and guest in-teract directly with each other. On these occasions, the host's orientation to his role as mediator becomes more overtly expressed as he struggles to regain his position and reaffirm his institutional identity as controller of the talk event.

It also seems that the way speakers design their questions can also function to construct different footings within this institutional context. Greater or lesser levels of formality in address and grammatical register can serve to build relative positions of power and status within the course of the talk. So, while the structural organisation of the talk, and consequently the position speakers are talking from, play a key role in accounting for the way question forms are designed, produced and responded to within that framework, there are ways in which callers can construct a rather different interactional footing for themselves, which can reduce the institutional asymmetry of the talk.

As a final word to this chapter, my analysis was based on a data corpus where the asymmetry between participants is particularly marked in many respects. Margaret Thatcher was prime minister at the time, a strong political figure in a position of authority. Many of the callers were young, and in terms of power and social status, the gap between questioner and questioned was wide. Although evidence from other radio phone-ins with a three-party participant structure from the same period tends to support these claims, we still need to find out whether this structure for the organisation of three-party phone-in talk still holds in other programmes where the social distance between participants might be less marked.

My data in the next chapter are also taken from a media context, news and political interviews, where the participants do have a more symmetrical status in terms of their institutional identities. In this chapter I will turn to the question of control in interview talk and, particularly, to an analysis of the kinds of discursive resources participants use to negotiate issues of sense and meaning.

NOTES

1. A version of this chapter has appeared in Discourse Studies 3 (1) 2001.
2. Although this programme was recorded some years ago, the format is still current in similar broadcasts today.
3. Telephone conversations have long been the focus of attention within conversation analysis, starting with Sacks' (1992) early accounts of calls to a suicide prevention centre. More recently calls to emergency services (Houtkoop-Steenstra, 1991; Zimmerman, 1992) and Hopper's (1992) work on telephone talk have provided detailed descriptions of how telephone call openings are organised.
4. These rules are that a summons answer sequence is non-terminal, that is something must follow. They are non-repeatable, the summoner is obligated to talk again and the answerer is obligated to listen (Schegloff, 1972).
5. There is clearly something more to be said about the relationship between how these callers' names become problematic for MT and the issue of ethnicity, but as this is not my main focus here, I simply note these as examples of trouble in establishing caller identity.
6. This kind of personal framing also occurs when lay participants take the floor in other forms of audience participation broadcasts (cf. Thornborrow, 1997).
7. Clayman (1992) has shown that in interview talk, interviewers' questions take a similarly extended form and can contain several propositions before they reach the question as such. Interviewees will also wait for the question to be produced before attempting to take a response turn.

5

♦

RESOURCES FOR CONTROL: DISCURSIVE STRATEGIES IN MEDIA INTERVIEWS

So far in this book I have been arguing that the relationship between a speaker's institutional identity and status, and the potential identities that they can take up discursively in the ongoing talk, may be approached partially in terms of who gets access to particular types of turns, and thus access to particular discursive actions. In many contexts for institutional interaction, some turn types are structurally available to some participants while being more difficult to access by others, so consequently the kinds of actions that can be accomplished in those turns are also asymmetrically distributed between the participants. In the previous chapter, through my analysis of calls to a phone-in programme, where the talk is mediated by a host, I showed how control of the talk event is partly achieved through the structure of turn taking and the participation framework of a call, arguing that the mediation of direct interaction between two of the three participants, and the organisation of the access to particular turn types, both reduce the potentially powerful discursive role of a caller as 'questioner'.

In this chapter, another type of mediated interaction will be the focus of analysis: the interview. Broadly speaking, news interviews are mediated talk events where the discursive identities of questioner and answerer are institutionally inscribed in the roles of 'interviewer' and 'interviewee'. Again, I explore how the structural organisation of interview talk makes different kinds of discursive positions available to the participants. But in contrast to the radio phone-in data, in this context the institutional identity of 'interviewer' and the discursive identity of 'questioner' are more congruent in terms of participant status than the caller/questioner identity discussed in chapter 4. In other words, the person doing the questions also occupies the institutional status of talk manager.

As talk events, media news interviews contrast with more conversational media settings for talk, in so far as participants in them very often have publicly, professionally marked status and identity. In other words, the professional news interviewer is often engaged with a professional interviewee (for example, politician, spokesperson or institutional representative of various kinds) rather than with the lay participant who may call in to the type of radio phone-in programme in the last chapter. There are of course some occasions where interviewees *are* members of the general public, and I will be arguing that participant status and identity can in some cases shape the kind of talk that is produced within the context of an interview. The data I draw on here are taken from a range of television and radio interviews, involving professional politicians as well as lay participants, which have been recorded during the period 1987 to the present time of writing.[1] I discuss various discursive strategies available to participants for getting things done in the course of an interview, such as getting questions answered, getting access to the floor and establishing issues of speaker meaning, or 'gist', and I focus particularly on the potential power of the formulation (Heritage and Watson, 1979; Heritage, 1985) as a key resource in interview talk. In the first part of the chapter I give a brief overview of the turn-taking system in news interviews, and describe the function of formulations as discursive actions in this context. I then go on to discuss how formulations are conventionally used by interviewers as a powerful resource in this specific institutional context for talk.

TURN STRUCTURE IN NEWS INTERVIEWS

The organisation of turn taking in news interviews has been described by Heritage and Greatbach (1991) as an institutionally specialised system. Briefly summarised, within this system participants restrict themselves to the production of questions and answers (thereby sustaining the event as an interview rather than a discussion); interviewees cannot open or close interviews, neither can they allocate next turns to speakers; interviewer questions are often designed to set an 'agenda', and sometimes lead interviewees to engage in quite complex evasive tactics within the constraints of a turn-taking system where they are positioned as responders. The allocation of turns is predetermined, in that the interviewer goes first and the interviewee goes second, and the turn types are also predetermined, as interviewers take the question turn, while interviewees take the response turn. In more than two-party interviews, the interviewer is generally also responsible for speaker selection, so in this and other ways interviewers act as managers of the talk, organising who speaks when.

Interviewees do not generally self select as next speakers; if they do, some explicit reference is made to this action, as the following extract illustrates:

Extract (1) AP:7.3.79

```
MW: Can I- can I say something abou[t this.]
IR:                                [yes in ]deed.
    (0.5)
MW: e:r (0.7) As (0.5)Frank (.) Longford knows so
    well .hh er my views ... ((continues))
```

(Heritage and Greatbach, 1991: 103)

MW's first turn in this sequence is an explicit bid for the next interviewee turn, which the interviewer then accepts. In the next example, where an interviewee self selects out of turn and, unlike the speaker in the previous extract, does no explicit prefacing of this as a marked action, their intervention is not acknowledged by the interviewer:

Extract (2) O'Leary FT/Granada/2/6/87

```
1. DH: [---] I think this change in the world situation=
2. IR: =right
3. DH: requires a change in policy (.) and I'm tragically
4.     disappointed that unlike the American government
5.     the British government will not change
6.     as the world changes
7. GH: but [that's-
8. IR:     [right (.) and we're going to have to leave this
9.     particular section there
```

In this extract, the interviewer is moving towards closing this particular sequence, as can be seen by her utterance 'right' (line 2 and again in line 8). When one of the interviewees self selects to take the floor out of turn without making an explicit bid for a next speaker turn (line 7) he gets no acknowledgment, and the interviewer continues to close the sequence. More usually though, and in line with the example given in extract (1), a self-selecting speaker who does explicitly make a bid for the next speaker position may simply have their access to that next turn delayed until a next interviewee turn position becomes available and they are nominated by the interviewer as next speaker. The following extract illustrates this type of delay:

Extract (3) O'Leary FT/Granada/2/6/87

```
 1. GH:    [---] I think if he has any sense of shame now left
 2.        at all (.)he ought now to stand down from his
 3.        present position
 4. DH: → can I answer that
 5. GH:    he is seeking to defend a programme of (.) it's
 6.        a matter of the utmost importance to the British
 7.        people [---]
 8.        (4 lines omitted)
 9.        the nation is entitled to know (.)why he's still
10.        there (.) defending this policy
11. IR: → right (.) well you (.) you (.) Denis Healey (.)
12.        you've heard the cry (.) resign resign (.)
13.        what's your answer
14. DH:    well I've heard that all through my life but [---]
```

Here, DH makes an explicit bid for the next interviewee turn (line 4), then gets selected as next speaker by the interviewer once GH has completed his turn (lines 11 to 13).

Once an interviewee has been allocated the floor as the ratified speaker, the length of their turn at talk can be extensive, and interviewees are often reluctant to relinquish that turn until they have finished making their point. Once they have gained ratified access to the floor, and in view of the fact that an interviewee answer turn conventionally consists of an extended turn at talk (that is, it extends over more than one turn construction unit), getting an interviewee to stop talking can sometimes be problematic for interviewers. In extract (4) below, it takes the interviewer four attempts to close down the current interviewee's turn (here the interviewee is former American Senator George McGovern):

Extract (4) O'Leary FT/Granada/2/6/87

```
 1. IR: right
 2. GM: let me just underscore something that I don't think
 3.     has been brought out here tonight
 4.     as much as it should have (.)
 5.     and that (.) that is the purpose of nuclear weapons
 6.     is not to use them (.) if they're ever used
 7.     on a major scale (.) all of the major countries
 8.     are going to largely disappear
 9. IR: right
10. GM: there won't be any Britain if there is a nuclear
11.     exchange involving Britain and the Soviet Union
12.     there won't be any Soviet Union either because
13.     it will mean that we're going to be involved in
14.     a major nuclear war that may spell the end
15.     of all of us
16. IR: right (.) Senator
17. GM: so the important thing is to pursue policies
18.     that will avoid that and it's in that area where
19.     economics and arms control and diplomacy and
20.     politics become more important than the
21.     exact size of the nuclear force
22. IR: Senator McGovern (.) just to put some of the
23.     points to our panel here [---]
```

In this sequence, the interviewee continues until his point is completed, ignoring the interviewer's attempts to close his turn and open the floor to members of the panel until he has finished what he set out to do at the beginning of his turn: 'let me just underscore something . . .' (line 2). Another example of this extended turn holding can be seen in extract (5), where interviewee Norman Tebbit does attend to the interviewer's question, but by making an explicit bid to continue:

Extract (5) White TWNW//BBC1//24/05/87

```
1. NT: [---] there's a very common expression which they use
2.     (.) the government doesn't care (.) [we've heard that ]
3. IR:                                     [that hurts does it]
4. NT: no (.) no let me go on (.) we've heard that said time
5.     and time again [---]
```

Tebbit's response turn at line 4 is however not simply a bid to continue, 'no no let me go on', his response is also an explicit orientation to the violative nature of the interviewer's question as an interruption, that is, it does not occur at a proper transition relevant place in relation to the ongoing turn. Tebbit recyles the overlapped stretch of talk in his prior interrupted turn at the beginning of his next one, thus doubly displaying the interviewer's question as violative by retrieving his line just at the point at which he was interrupted[2] and holding on to his right to continue the turn as current selected speaker.

So within the basic constraints of the turn-taking system in news interviews, where the interviewer does the questions and the interviewee is under an obligation to provide a recognisable response to those questions, all participants can be seen to use a range of strategies to deal with whatever may occur during the course of an interview. Once an interviewee takes a response turn, they can exercise the right to 'go on'; in multi-party interviews, they can make explicit requests for the floor rather than wait for the interviewer to select them as next speaker. Interviewers, on the other hand, as well as doing the questioning, have to manage the openings, closings and transitions between speakers. While openings are usually relatively straightforward matters, closings and transitions can require some quite complex work as we have seen in the examples above.[3]

As well as occupying the role of talk managers, in terms of determining who speaks when, interviewers also have resources for directing the content of interview talk. There are discursive strategies which can be brought to bear on issues of meaning, when 'sense' is being interactively negotiated between participants, and in the broad context of media news interviews, including interviews with both political experts and lay interviewees, the formulation is one such strategy. Since formulating plays a central role in the sequential management and establishment of gist, it is a key interviewer resource. In the next section I describe the role of formulations in news interviews and give some specific examples to illustrate ways in which they can function as a powerful strategy in interview talk.

FORMULATIONS

In conversation, speaker meaning is not always direct and transparent and thus can be subject to routine checks by participants in the talk. One way that speakers do this kind of meaning-check is through using formulations. A formulation, then, is a particular type of third-turn receipt of information, which has been produced for one speaker by another and which functions to establish the gist, or the 'for-all-practical-purposes definiteness of sense', of what has been said in the prior turn (Heritage and Watson, 1979: 137). During any stretch of talk, speakers can produce glosses of utterances which are 'multi-implicative', that is, utterances which may be in need of clarification or which are open to a range of interpretations. Formulating actions display which of these interpretations is being taken up by a recipient, which can then be confirmed or disconfirmed by the next speaker. Heritage and Watson describe the function of formulating utterances as follows:

The primary businesss of formulations is to demonstrate understanding and presumptively, to have that understanding attended to, and as a first preference, endorsed.   (1979: 138)

A formulation makes up the first part of an adjacency pair, in so far as it will give rise to a second-part response, either a confirmation (described as the 'first preference' by Heritage and Watson above) or a disconfirmation. The formulation–dis/confirmation adjacency pair sequence is therefore an important mechanism through which participants can jointly negotiate and display decisions about sense in their talk; in other words, it is a way of establishing gist as the talk proceeds. Heritage gives the extract below (taken from a street interview with a Welshman) as an illustration of one type of formulating activity:

Extract (5) WAO: King of Wales

```
Int:    Would you be happy to see Prince Charles become
        King of Wales?
Man:    heh Well I:(h) cou(h)ld(h)n' I- you know I just
        couldn't care tup↑pence who comes King and who
        don't like
        (0.5)
Int: →  You don't think it makes any difference to you.
Man:    No::.=Not one bit. (.) Not one bit. (0.2) Same
        (weelbeein) anyway.
```

(Heritage, 1985: 105–6)

The interviewer here re-presents the statement made in the prior turn, slightly shifting its meaning through inferential elaboration: 'You don't think it makes any difference to you.' The interviewee's response is an emphatic confirmation of this new formulation of his statement: 'No. Not one bit.' The topic is thus maintained as a focus for the talk over a further two turns, and in the process, as Heritage points out, a two turn question–answer sequence is developed into a short interview.

Another example of how formulating functions to develop issues of sense between participants can be seen in the next extract taken from a phone-in on housing provision. Here, the host takes on the role of making a meaning explicit for the purposes of a third party to the talk, housing minister at the time Sir George Younger:

Extract (6) Ross BBCR4/Housing/09/95

```
1. Host:   Kim is not saying that abuse doesn't occasionally
2.         take place (.) if I understand you correctly Kim
3.         you're saying that this is being used (.) as an
4.         excuse=
5. Caller:       =yes=
6. Host:          =to inflame emotions that one group is
7.         being set against another an'I an'I wonder whether
8.         Sir George you'd like to take up (.) Kim's invitation
9.         to (.) and repudiate the sort of language [---]
```

In lines 1–4 of this extract the host uses an extended formulation to establish a prior speaker's meaning for a third party (here Sir George Younger). The caller then briefly confirms (line 5) the host's interpretation of the gist of what she has just said in a previous turn, and he then goes on to invite the guest to respond to this newly clarified issue, thus refocusing the content of the talk for the next speaker's turn.

The business of establishing direction and sense in talk can be a delicate matter, particularly in view of the claim that the preferred response to a formulation is a confirmation. This would suggest that disconfirmations will involve more work on the part of the responding party, and may be a cause of potential trouble. While in conversational contexts for talk formulating activity may be a symmetrical affair, with any participant able to pursue the gist of a prior turn through a formulation, in institutional contexts the distribution of turn types between participants usually results in some speakers occupying the role of 'formulator' while others find themselves taking up the position of 'responder'. Drew (2001) has noted that formulations actually appear to be relatively rare phenomena in the available conversational data corpora of CA; whereas they occur frequently as features of institutional talk, and particularly in the context of news interviews.

Typically, it is questioners who occupy the formulating role. In institutional interaction, then, it is likely that formulations and their responses may turn out to be the potentially critical sites for participants' struggles over meaning and sense to be played out.

FORMULATIONS AND RECEIPT OF 'NEWS' IN INTERVIEWS

In conversational contexts for talk where 'news' is information that has been solicited by a prior question, the news eliciting and news providing question/answer sequence is usually followed by a third-turn receipt of that news (Jefferson, 1981; Schegloff, 1982). This is illustrated in the extracts below:

Extract (7)

```
A:    how's yer foot
B:    oh it's healing beautifully
A: →  good
```

Extract (8)

```
M:    how many cigarettes yih had
E:    none
M: →  oh really
E:    no
M:    very good
```

(Heritage, 1985: 98)

The arrowed turns contain a third-turn receipt token; in extract (7) this is an assessment 'good', and in extract (8) a newsmark 'oh really'. Heritage (1985) has argued that these third-turn receipt tokens function to 'align the questioner to the answerer as a recipient of reported information' (p. 98) and that they generally indicate some form of commitment on behalf of the news recipient to the truth, or adequacy, of the information received. In institutional contexts such as courtroom cross examinations (Atkinson and Drew, 1979) or broadcast news interviews (Heritage, 1985), which involve talk produced for an overhearing audience[4] (respectively the judge and jury, and the listening/viewing audience), conversation analysts have found that such alignments in third-turn receipts of news are rare. These analyses have shown how by avoiding the production of receipt tokens, the questioner or interviewer is able to decline the role of report recipient, while maintaining the role of report elicitor. Furthermore, the issue of recipient alignment to the previous utterance as adequate and true is also avoided, thereby allowing the recipient to remain in a more neutral position *vis-à-vis* the news they have just elicited.

FORMULATIONS AND INSTITUTIONAL NEUTRALITY

It has been claimed that because of the requirement for public broadcasting institutions to remain unbiased and neutral in their reporting of news, alignment to interviewee utterances is something that news interviewers avoid. Steven Clayman (1992) has argued that 'neutrality . . . is a particularly pressing issue for those who interview for television' (p. 163) and that news interviewers 'systematically refrain from aligning with or against the opinions they report' (p. 174). Most often, rather than producing a next turn receipt which commits them to some form of personal alignment in relation to the statement just made, interviewers have other strategies for maintaining a more neutral footing, as can be seen in the next two examples:

Extract (9) (MacNeil/Lehrer 6/10/85a:CT:4)

```
IR: But isn't this- uh::: critics uh on thuh conservative- side
    of thuh political argument have argued that this is:. abiding
    by the treaty is:. unilateral
```

(Clayman, 1992: 171)

Extract (10) Humphrys/Hague BBCR4/TP/5/99

```
WH: so I don't think there can be much argument about that
    there's only one party in this election making big gains
    (.) and that's the conservative [(party)]
IR:                                 [on the ]other hand if you look
    at shares of the vote and all of that (.) Labour's still ahead of
    you and it's the first time I think it was Margaret Becket who
    pointed this out it's the first time this century that any that
    any government has been ahead of the opposition in the mid
    term ele:ctions
```

The interviewers in these two examples both dispute the point just made, but they do so by attributing the grounds of the disagreement to someone else. In extract (9) the interviewer starts off with an interrogative, but then self-repairs to attribute the view to 'critics on the conservative side'. In extract (10), the interviewer begins by taking issue with the previous claim, then similarly embeds a third-party source into his opposing statement, 'Margaret Becket who pointed this out', before repeating 'it's the first time' and continuing his turn. By using this strategy, both interviewers explicitly avoid ownership of a contesting statement and saying 'on record' anything that could be attributed to their own point of view.

Another strategy for avoiding third-turn alignment with news is to replace conversational receipt tokens, such as 'oh' or 'really', with formulations. In the context of news interviews, formulations take the form of glosses, summaries and developments of the gist of interviewee utterances, and it has been argued that they are addressed as much to the overhearing audience as they are to the direct recipient of the formulation, the interviewee (Heritage, 1985). In this way, the alignment of the relationship between the interviewer as questioner, and the interviewee as answerer, is altered so as to bring the audience into the participatory frame as report recipients. To use Goffman's terms, the participation framework of a news interview consists of a report elicitor (the interviewer), a report producer (the interviewee) and report receivers (the non-co-present, indirectly targeted audience); this framework, and the discursive identities constituted in it, is interactionally aligned to by the participants through the design of their talk. In news interviews, then, formulations are a key discursive resource through which interviewers are able to maintain their own role as report elicitor and that of the audience as report receiver.

The formulations produced by interviewers in their third receipt turns can function in several ways. Firstly, they can be used as prompts to either clarify interviewee reports, or to refocus and/or redirect them, often according to the newsworthiness of certain aspects of the report. Heritage summarises this prompting function as follows:

> Formulations advance the prior report by finding a point in the prior utterance and thus shifting its focus, redeveloping its gist, making something explicit that was previously implicit in the prior utterance, or by making inferences about its presuppositions or implications. (1985: 104)

One illustration of this was given in extract (5), where the interviewer formulates the interviewee's answer, 'I just couldn't care tuppence who comes King', as 'You don't think it makes any difference to you.' He thereby makes the interviewee's meaning explicit by recycling an implicit proposition from his prior turn.

A second function of interviewer formulations can be seen in extract (11), where interviewer Nick Ross is talking to former Alliance politician John Cartwright about defence policy:[5]

Extract (11) Ross WP/C4/29/05/87

```
JC:    but one shouldn't run away with the idea that there's vast
       sums of money to be saved eliminating those commitments (.)
       they don't actually cost vast sums of money
IR: →  but that's something Alliance would be prepared to do.
```

Here, the interviewer is again making an inferential statement based on the content of the previous turn, but the nature of this formulation is what Heritage describes as an 'elaborative probe'. Rather than giving rise to confirmations, as we saw in Heritage's example in extract (5), these kind of formulations tend to produce more elaborate answers from interviewees. Here is the response Ross gets from Cartwright:

Extract (12) Ross WP/C4/29/05/87

```
IR: → but that's something Alliance would be
        prepared to do.
JC:     I think that if one- (.) we are committed
        to a total re-examination of the defence budget
        to make sure that the commitments marry up
        with the resources available (.) and the
        first thing one has to look at is the outer
        area activities (.) but as I say (.) I don't
        think you're going to save vast sums of money
        in looking at those.
```

This response is not a straightforward confirmation or disconfirmation of the proposition contained in the formulation, but a response which develops the topic of 'outer area commitments' without either agreeing or disagreeing with the interviewer's formulation. The interviewee here begins his response turn by 'I think that if one-' but then repairs this to what appears to be a more general statement of policy 'we are committed . . .'. This type of response falls into the category of what Sandra Harris (1991) terms a type B 'indirect' answer, that is, one which maintains the cohesion, topical coherence and presuppositionl framework of the question, but from which a direct 'yes' or 'no' cannot be inferred.

Interviewer formulations can therefore function either as prompts or as probes to elicit more talk from an interviewee, often in clarification of the meaning contained in a part or the whole of their previous turn. In both cases, they give rise to a further response from the interviewee, which can be either a confirmation/disconfirmation, or a more elaborate and often less direct answer.

FORMULATIONS AS AN INTERVIEWER RESOURCE

As I have already noted, in news interviews, turns are distributed such that it is the interviewer who is in the position of doing the formulating, while the interviewee is in the position of doing the responding. This asymmetrical distribution of turns has a significant consequence, in so far as the ability to re-orient and direct the topic, or content of the talk, lies primarily (although not entirely) with the interviewer. In their third-turn position as formulator, interviewers can paraphrase information given by interviewees, make implicit propositions explicit, and select certain elements of an interviewee's talk as worthy of pursuit while discarding others. As well as serving as a convenient resource for maintaining a footing of neutrality, formulating has also been described as 'a weapon in the news interviewer's armoury' (Heritage, 1985:

114), enabling interviewers to maintain the discursive upper hand while at the same time engaging in the institutionally legitimate activity of clarifying matters for the audience.

To summarise this discussion of news interviews so far, the potential of formulations as a powerful resource for the interviewer can be described as operating on two levels. The first is through a structurally asymmetrical relationship in the talk where the interviewer is in the discursive role of questioner and formulator, while the interviewee is in the role of answerer and under a strong obligation to respond to interviewer formulations. The second is in the degree of control a formulator may be able to exercise over the orientation and content of the talk. It is open to interviewers either to respond co-operatively to statements made by the interviewee, or to resist and challenge those statements in their third turn receipt of the information they elicit. Both types of receipt can be accomplished through formulating activity, while at the same time preserving the neutrality required by national broadcasting institutions.

CONTROLLING THE AGENDA: GETTING AN ANSWER

Interviewers can exercise control as questioners by ensuring that interviewees provide adequate answers. David Greatbach (1986) has observed that interviewers try to hold interviewees accountable by keeping them 'on topic' and not letting them move too far away from the agenda established by the interviewer. In contrast to the early days of broadcasting, where political interviews were marked by a deferential attitude towards interviewees who by and large could ignore the agendas set by the interviewer, current interviewing practice is to hold the interviewee to answering the question. Interviewees have in turn had to find ways around this and to develop strategies for resisting interviewers' agendas without being perceived as being evasive.[6] Interviewers are however still in the position of being able to challenge interviewees, whom they consider are avoiding giving an adequate answer, by explicitly drawing attention to this avoidance. The next extract taken from a TV interview with former conservative politician John Stanley, again on the topic of defence, illlustrates this type of challenge:

Extract (13) Ross WP/C4/29/05/87

```
 1. NR:  →  [OK let me put my question]
 2. JS:     [so the Soviets have      ] come to the conclusion
 3. NR:  →  [my question ]to you again because in truth you know=
 4. JS:     [the Soviets-]
 5. NR:  →  =you're not [tackling my question ]
 6. JS:                 [the Soviets have made] it quite clear
 7.         that for them now at last it is worth their
 8.         while to come back to the negotiating table
 9. NR:     look (.) I want to give you the opportunity
10.         to answer that question because I think it's
11.         in your own interests to do so [---]
```

Stanley's pursuit of his topic (lines 2 and 4) leads to an explicit accusation by Ross 'you're not tackling my question' (line 5). The amount of overlap occurring in this sequence also increases the confrontational nature of the exchange, with the participants recycling the overlapped stretch of their turn three times before the trouble is resolved and Stanley succeeds in completing his point (the overlap occurs from line 1 to line 6). But Ross takes up the issue of the unanswered question again at line 9, with an emphatic turn-initial 'look', making it clear that Stanley has not yet produced an adequate answer. Control of the topical agenda and getting a question answered can therefore become areas of interactional conflict betwen participants in interview talk where struggles such as the one played out in extract (13) occur. In the last resort, when interviewees continue to resist, then interviewers can insist, as can be seen in Ross's treatment of Stanley above.

'SO YOU'RE SAYING': GETTING THE SENSE

The second way in which interviewers can control the direction of the talk is through their role as formulators. I now turn to some more specific examples of how interviewers use formulating as a resource for holding interviewees to addressing questions of sense and meaning and for exerting control over the direction of the talk.

Many formulations are structurally identifiable not just by their occurrence in third turn receipt positions, but also by a prefacing frame which has a recurring identifiable syntactic form [(so) + you + verbal/mental process token]. Interviewers often preface the formulation of the gist of a prior utterance with 'so you're saying that . . .', 'so you're suggesting that . . .' or 'so you think that . . .'. Sometimes they use phrases like 'in other words . . .'. These phrases tie the upcoming formulation to what the interviewee has just said in the prior turn by explicitly attributing the content of the interviewer turn to the previous speaker. Not all issues of gist and sense are necessarily dealt with through formulations, and interviewers can elaborate on meaning without using a 'so you're saying x' frame, as we can see in this exchange between interviewer Nick Ross and former Alliance politician John Cartwright:

Extract (14) Ross WP/C4/29/05/87

```
JC: I think the first area one examines
    are the outer area commitments (.)
    the commitments beyond the European theatre
IR: the Falklands (.) Belize (.) places like that
JC: exactly
```

These types of meaning development sequences are co-operative in the sense that some element in the prior turn has been identified by the interviewer as a possible source of trouble for the audience, and becomes the object of a clarificatory repair sequence. Here, 'outer area commitments beyond the European theatre' is one such element which gets picked up by the interviewer as in need of such clarification. His gloss of this phrase, which specifies 'the Falklands (.) Belize' is then confirmed by the interviewee: 'exactly'. A potentially problematic issue of meaning has thus been dealt with successfully and uncontentiously between the interviewer and interviewee for the viewing and listening audience.[7]

Rather less co-operative is a different type meaning check in third turn receipts which Heritage (1985) has defined as 'the inferentially elaborative probe'. As we saw in extract (5), these 'probes' are produced when interviewers make an interpretive inference about a presupposition, or an implication, based on a statement contained in the prior turn, but they are not repairs like the clarification in extract (14). Instead, they can often be used to challenge an interviewee's response. The difference between the type of co-operative clarification exemplified in (14) and a challenging formulation is illustrated in this next extract, an exchange between former US Senator Richard Perle and interviewer Olivia O'Leary:

Extract (15) O'Leary FT/Granada/2/6/87

```
1. RP:     [---] it will be awfully difficult to explain that
2.         to Americans who are otherwise asked to bear
3.         enormous risks (.) even though it may be in our
4.         interests to bear those risks
5. IR: →   but but you still can't say that what the labour
6.         party is telling the electorate is wrong (.)
7.         basically
8.         [--- (3 lines omitted)]
9.         but there will still be the United States nuclear
10.        umbrella there to fend off any threat (.)
11.        any blackmail (.) from the Soviet Union (.)
12.    →   and you're really not suggesting that he's wrong
13. RP: →  no I'm saying that the first statement is the only
14.        one that the labour party is in a position to make
15.        [---]
```

In a previous question turn (before we join the talk in the transcript) O'Leary has asked Perle whether a non-nuclear Britain could take refuge under an American 'nuclear umbrella'. Her receipt of his response (line 5) elaborates a possible inferential meaning using the explicit formulation structure 'but you still can't say . . .', followed by a restatement of that inference later in the same turn (line 12): 'you're really not suggesting that he's wrong'. Perle's response is a disconfirmation: 'no I'm saying that . . .'. This type of inferentially elaborative formulation tends to be received by interviewees as a challenge to their position, and is frequently followed by a disconfirmation, as happens here, and a further restatement of the point. In political interviews, then, the principal interactive function of inferentially elaborative probes seems to be to challenge interviewee answers rather than to endorse them.

Another type of formulation involves the 'recycling' of a proposition contained in an interviewee's utterance (Heritage, 1985). In a recycle, interviewers paraphrase, gloss or make explicit some proposition contained in the prior turn, rather than making an interpretive inference based on it. Recycles can be used either co-operatively or unco-operatively. The next extract illustrates a co-operative recycle, and is taken from a BBC radio phone-in about the provision of council housing in Britain. The host Nick Ross is talking to a caller about her views on whether such housing should be funded by 'the taxpayer':

Extract (16) Ross BBCR4/Housing/09/95

```
 1. Host:      [---]                                 d'you think
 2.            it's ethically right that taxpayers should be
 3.            expected to find you a home for the rest of your
 4.            life
 5. Caller:    for a long time I was a taxpayer and (.) things (.)
 6.            .hh which I had some contribution towards (.)
 7.            matters that I had some contribution towards (.)
 8.            went very wrong for me [.h ] erm [and   my child]
 9. Host:   →                        [mmm]     [so it i- so it]
10. Caller:    yes=
11. Host:        =it is right=
12. Caller:              =it is right (.) yes it is right
13.            it is the safety net that (.) is there and I would
14.            like to see it continue [to be there
```

The host's third turn receipt of the caller's answer (line 9) is an inferential elaboration of the proposition contained in her utterance in lines 5–7, i.e. that when she had been a taxpayer, she had contributed towards such things. She pre-empts the complete utterance 'it is right' by responding to the host's overlapped formulating turn 'so it i-' (line 9) with 'yes', then by an emphatic repeat of this formulation, 'it is right', and continues with an even stronger statement of her position (lines 13 and 14).

A similar kind of co-operative formulation occurs in extract (17), taken from the same programme:

Extract (17) Ross BBCR4/Housing/09/95

```
Caller:    people have been coming into these flats (.)
           um single people (1.0) uh with no priorities (0.7)
           an' they've been getting ground floor flats
Host:    → so you think people are jumping the queue
Caller:  → they are definitely jumping the queue
```

The interviewer here recycles an implicit proposition contained in the prior caller turn: 'so you think people are jumping the queue', which gets a subsequent strong confirmation by the caller. In both these extracts, clarification of speaker meaning is jointly and co-operatively produced by host and caller through a two-stage sequence of question and answer, formulation and confirmation. These sequences, although typical of news interview interaction, clearly do not only occur in interviews. They are also observable in other contexts for mediated interaction (in this case a radio phone-in) where question/answer sequences are developed into extended exchanges between participants, whose identities as questioners and answerers are institutionally differentiated, and where the talk is being produced for an overhearing audience.

To return to the context of political interviews, the recycling formulation can again function either co-operatively or unco-operatively. In the following examples,

extract (18) illustrates a co-operative use of the recycle in an exchange between interviewer Olivia O'Leary and former US Senator George McGovern, while extract
(19), taken from an interview by Nick Ross with Labour politician Denzil Davies,
illustrates an unco-operative, challenging recyle.

Extract (18) O'Leary FT/Granada/2/6/87

```
1. GM: [---] whether Britain has nuclear forces or not
2.      on its own territory has very little to do
3.      with America's recognition of our mutual interest
4.      (.) and the defence of Europe
5. IR: but a Britain which was no longer a nuclear power
6. →    (.) you say that it will still be regarded (.)
7.      as it always has been (.) as an important ally
8. GM: but of course
```

The interviewer here paraphrases the gist of McGovern's prior turn (lines 5–7), and
her recycling of his account of America's view of Britain gets confirmed in his next
turn 'but of course' (line 8). The point McGovern is making has then been clarified
co-operatively between the two participants in this exchange. This is not the case in
the next extract, where the interviewer Nick Ross uses a recycle unco-operatively to
challenge a point being made by the interviewee Denzil Davies:

Extract (19) Ross WP/C4/29/05/87

```
1. IR: → now this is fascinating (.) you're saying
2.      that you're trying to allay groundless
3.      fears(.) all this taxpayer's money (.)
4.      which we could spend on other things (.)
5.      you're going to put into conventional
6.      armaments (.) to allay groundless fears
7. DD: → no   (.) it's not the case of the fears
8.      being groundless (.) the fears are [still there
9. IR:                                      [I'm sorry but
10.     that was your phrase
```

Here, the interviewer uses a recycle to challenge a proposition contained in Davies's
prior extended turn, where he has been arguing that it is necessary to maintain
conventional weapons in Europe. Furthermore, he prefaces his formulating turn
with an assessment 'now this is fascinating'. Without going into greater detail here,
we can see that this interviewer turn is from the outset being built as a challenging
receipt of Davies's response. Ross's use of 'fascinating' is hearably ironic, and he
goes on to select one element from Davies's prior turn, when he states that 'the fears
may be groundless (.) but the fears are still there', and recycles it as 'you're saying that
you're trying to allay groundless fears'. This formulation is received by Davies as a
challenge to his point, which he disconfirms in his next turn (line 7). Ross then responds with a justification of his recycle in a 'your-words-not-mine' claim: 'that was
your phrase' (line 10). Although the use of this claim here, following up a formulation

turn, may function to reinforce the interviewer's construction of his footing as institutionally 'neutral' in relation to an interviewee statement, and to distance him from
both authorship as well as principal of the utterance (Goffman, 1981), it also contributes to the very challenging nature of the interviewer's talk, and, as we will see
shortly, it precedes a continuing series of formulations by the interviewer resulting
in a confrontational sequence in which Davies is put in the position of having to
repeatedly disconfirm the unco-operative recycling of his utterances by Ross.

The next extract, which contains an extended sequence of interviewer formulation and interviewee disconfirmation turns, is a further illustration of this challenging turn design from the same interview between Nick Ross and Denzil Davies.
The beginning of the sequence has already been given as extract (19), but I include
it to show the whole sequence here.

Extract (20) Ross FT/C4/29/05/87

```
 1. IR: now this is fascinating (.) you're saying
 2.     that you're trying to allay groundless
 3.     fears (.) all this taxpayer's money (.)
 4.     which we could spend on other things (.)
 5.     you're going to put into conventional
 6.     armaments (.) to allay groundless fears
 7. DD: no (.) it's not the case of the fears being
 8.     groundless (.) the fears are [still there
 9. IR:                              [I'm sorry but
10.     that was your phrase
11. DD: the fears are still there (.) perhaps less
12.     in Britain than in Germany (.) I talk to
13.     members of both [parties-
14. IR:                 [so we're doing it for the
15.     Germans
16. DD: no we are not (.) we are doing it to get
17.     rid of nuclear weapons because they are
18.     dangerous and they would destroy Europe
19.     if they were used
20. IR: ah so it's the price (.) [the price-
21. DD:                          [to some extent
22.     yes (.) the price to be paid for getting
23.     rid of nuclear weapons is to increase the
24.     conventional forces
25. IR: the electoral price (.) in other words the
26.     voters couldn't stomach reducing conventional
27.     forces [and-
28. DD:       [it's not a question of voting (.)
29.     it's a proper price to pay to get rid of more
30.     dangerous weapons because we need to increase
31.     our conventional forces [---]
```

As we have already seen, Ross's first turn in this sequence (line 1) is a recycle of a
statement Davies has made in the prior turn, which is then disconfirmed by the
interviewee. The next three interviewer turns are further inferentially elaborative

formulations (lines 14, 20 and 25) which are dealt with in turn by the interviewee. The first of these unco-operative formulations, 'so we're doing it for the Germans', is emphatically denied by Davies (line 16). However, after Ross's next formulation, 'ah so it's the price-', Davies interrupts (line 21) with, 'to some extent yes'. This interruption has two potentially advantageous consequences for the interviewee: first, it enables him to respond before an inferential statement has actually been formulated and, second, it enables him to treat the upcoming formulation as a co-operative one and produce a confirmation in that response. Davies anticipates the content of Ross's next formulating turn (recognisable as such through its recurring format 'ah so it's the price') and interrupts at that point, before Ross has produced what turns out to be another unco-operative inferential formulation. He is thus able to align himself with the interviewer's anticipated formulation rather than against it, and continue with a positive response, 'yes (.) the price to be paid for getting rid of nuclear weapons', rather than a negative one as he has done in the previous two responses. Ross then engages in a counter-move by leaving Davies's confirmatory response unacknowledged and repairing the interrupted formulation of his previous turn. He recycles 'the price', repaired as 'the electoral price', which enables him to reverse Davies's momentary advantage and to put him again into the position of having to disconfirm another unco-operative formulation, 'in other words the voters couldn't stomach reducing conventional forces'. Once again, Davies does not wait for him to finish, but interrupts (line 28) with, 'it's not a question of voting'.

In this extract, where almost every interviewer turn contains an unco-operative formulation, the interaction becomes more confrontational. In news interviews it is normally the case that interviewers and interviewees wait for each other to finish a turn by producing respectively a recognisably complete question or answer (Heritage and Greatbach, 1991). In extract (20) both Ross and Davies interrupt each other rather than waiting for a potential completion point in a prior turn before taking the floor. The degree of conflict is also heightened through the number of disconfirmations Davies has to produce in response to Ross's repeated unco-operative formulations. In this case then, formulation is used by the interviewer to pursue a particular unfavourable interpretation of the interviewee's statements through a series of unco-operative moves. As a result, the interviewee is put at an interactional disadvantage in so far as he has to deal with that interpretation in a disconfirming response, rather than developing his own argument.

Heritage has claimed that unco-operative formulations do not necessarily disadvantage the interviewee, they only give rise to disconfirmations:

The unco-operative character of these sequences arises from the fact that, whether inadvertently or by design, the interviewer formulates a version of the interviewee's position that the latter might be expected to deny [. . .] just as a co-operative formulation may occur as a component in a sequence that is ultimately damaging to an interviewee's position, so an interviewee may benefit from the opportunity to reject a particular version of his position.
(1985: 112)

While the question of ultimate advantage or disadvantage to any given interviewee, as a result of interviewer formulating actions, is not one that can really be resolved here, it does seem to be the case that one consequence of a high frequency of unco-operative formulations on the part of the interviewer in political interviews is that the interview becomes noticeably more confrontational. If an interviewer's third-turn receipt activity consists mainly of unco-operative formulation of the gist of the interviewee's prior turn, then the interviewee is put in the position of repeatedly having to disconfirm the propositions that constitute that activity. The issue of gist, then, becomes foregrounded as a conflict over what exactly an interviewee might be saying and meaning. The conflict involves an increase in the amount of work interviewees have to do in their response turns in order to resist the development of these inter-viewer-produced meanings; resistance which has in the first instance to be achieved through negating a proposition already on the floor, before producing a new one.

From the evidence in the data discussed here, I suggest that interviewers do indeed use unco-operative formulations by design in order to challenge inter-viewees and put them under some pressure to respond to those formulations of gist, in other words, to confirm or disconfirm possible glosses or inferential interpreta-tions of their statements.

INTERVIEWEE RESISTANCE: STRIKING BACK

Greatbach (1993) has noted that the style of interviewing has evolved from the deferential to the critical, and that over the years there have been occasions (some now notorious in the history of interviewing) when an interviewee has walked off the set in protest at the interviewer's questions,[8] or when an interviewer has per-sisted in asking exactly the same question over and over again until he got an answer. Individual interviewers can build reputations on their interview technique and style. Extract (21) is taken from BBC Radio 4's 'Start the Week', when Jeremy Paxman was interviewing former US Secretary of State Henry Kissinger among his guests on the programme:

Extract (21) Paxman STW/BBCR4/28/06/99

```
 1. Ir:  can we t'ba- turn to Indo-China for which you (.)
 2.      t- received the Nobel peace prize in 1973 that (.)
 3.      deal did not bring peace to Indo-China m.hhh (.)
 4.      was there any part of you felt a fraud in accepting
 5.      it↑
 6. Kis: (ye-) felt a what↑
 7. IR:  a fraud in accepting the Nobel peace prize
 8. Kis: I wonder what you do when you do a uh (.) a
 9.      hostile interview=
10. IR:                   =uh hu ((slight laugh))
11.      I was merely trying to explore↓
12. Kis: em [yeah
13. IE:     [this is mr Paxman being very kind↓
```

This brief metadiscursive interlude, emerging within the question/answer sequenc-ing of the interview when Kissinger initiates a request for clarification (line 6), nicely illustrates the participants' knowledge of Paxman's reputation as a tough interviewer.[9] Kissinger's comment (lines 8 and 9) and another participant's ironic evaluation of Paxman's questioning on this occasion as 'very kind' (line 13) highlight both the critical tone of the interview, while demonstrating an awareness that the strategies Paxman is using on this occasion are nevertheless quite restrained. This interview in fact contained very few unco-operative interviewer formulations.

In the concluding part of this chapter I want to look at two final examples of how interviewees respond to formulations as challenging moves, and the strategies they use for dealing with interviewers' attempts to select and interpret elements of their talk in unco-operative, or 'hostile' (to use Kissinger's term) third turns. Both are taken from political interviews. Extract (22) is from a TV interview with former conservative government minister Norman Tebbit, and the question relates to what became known in the 1987 British general election campaign as the 'Falklands Factor'. During this campaign, the conservative party claimed that they would be the party to best defend the national interests. Tebbit is engaged in avoiding a direct response to the interviewer's question 'are you suggesting that the labour party . . . is not patriotic'. The transcript begins at the concluding point of his extended answer to that question:

Extract (22) White TWNW/BBC1/24/05/87

```
 1. NT: [---] any of us who have had experience in
 2.      government (.) particularly in the cabinet
 3.      (.) know that it is not always easy to get
 4.      full agreement on an issue (.) even amongst
 5.      people of the same party
 6. IR: but are you telling me that it's in the
 7.      patriotic national interest that the tories
 8.      should have a large majority
 9. NT: I think (.) my own view is that it is in
10.      the national interest that the tories
11.      should have a large majority but
12.      I don't claim it's a matter of patriotism
13.      over that (.) of course not
```

In his formulation in line 6, White is making an inferential interpretation based on a claim in Tebbit's prior turn relating to the the benefits of having a large conservative majority in parliament. The formulation is framed as a question here, 'are you telling me', and Tebbit deals with it as such. Rather than simply confirming or disconfirming the inferred proposition, 'it's in the patriotic national interest that the tories should have a large majority', he is able to split his response into both a positive and a negative answer. If we compare this to the type of formulating actions in extract (20), where the interviewee responds to a series of interviewer recycles with disconfirmations, Tebbit's response seems a more productive way of dealing with the interviewer's formulation, through his receipt of it as a question rather than as an assertion to be denied or confirmed. In this way he is able to maintain a positive alignment with part of the interviewer's question, 'my own view is that it *is* in the national interest', while distancing himself from the 'patriotic interest' claim.

A similar strategy is used by the interviewee in extract (23), where Ross is questioning alliance politician John Cartwright about nuclear defence policy:

Extract (23) Ross WP/C4/29/05/87

```
JC: [---] and the first thing one has to look at
    is the outer area activities (.) but as I say
    I don't think you're going to save
    vast sums of money in looking at those
IR: so alliance commitment (.)if you think of Britain
    as a world policeman (.) alliance would presumably
    like to see Britain upholding the weak against bullies
    all around the world (.) you're saying well (.)
    we're not going to
JC: I think our role as an independent world
    policeman was completed a long time ago [---]
```

This time it is the interviewee, Cartwright, who takes up an element of the interviewer turn, and rather than explicitly confirm or deny the formulated proposition 'we're not going to uphold the weak against bullies', slightly shifts the focus of the talk. By taking issue with Ross's metaphoric representation of Britain as a 'world policeman', Cartwright is denying the grounds on which the formulation is built, thus weakening its force as a challenging move on the part of the interviewer. He is then able to continue the remainder of his turn by talking about the role of the United Nations in maintaining world peace. These interviewee strategies seem more successful as resistance to interviewer formulations than those used by Denzil Davies in extract (20).

CONCLUSIONS

In this chapter I have discussed the function of formulations and other discursive resources that are available to participants in news interviews. I have shown how in this context, as in the radio phone-in programme, the structural organisation of the talk, and the specialised system of turn-taking of interview interaction, make certain turn types and positions available to some participants and not to others. In their institutional role as managers of the talk event, interviewers ask the questions, select who speaks when, determine whether a question has been answered adequately and decide when to end an interview; in their interactional role, from their position of news receivers within the interview turn-taking system, they are able to use formulations either co-operatively or unco-operatively in the third-turn receipt of news. Interviewers, then, are in a strong position to control the direction of the talk in terms of what happens in the next interviewee turn, as well as by selecting particular meanings from a prior interviewee turn and making them salient. Sometimes these selections can have a clarifying function, but in political interviewing they are often received as challenges to an interviewee's position and produce disconfirmations in the next turn. On the other hand, interviewees have resources for holding the floor, resisting interviewer agendas and dealing with unco-operative formulations. One such resource in response to unco-operative formulating is to build responses which avoid direct disconfirmation of the previous turn, as we saw in the last two extracts discussed above.

Control of the talk in this institutional context, then, is something which is constantly shifting and negotiable in the course of the interview. Since the social relationship between interviewers and interviewees may often be more symmetrical than is the case in some of the other institutional data I have analysed, with participants occupying different institutional roles but having similar professional status, the potential power of their respective interactional positions, and the discursive resources of control and resistance that they mobilise from within those positions, become more salient and observable as key strategies in the interplay between questioners and answerers in news interviews.

To illustrate this point, I end the chapter with a recent account in the British press of an incident that took place during the course of an interview between the TV broadcaster and political interviewer, Sir Robin Day,[10] and former prime minister Margaret Thatcher:

Once, asked if she intended to sack certain ministers, she replied: 'You are going further than I wish to go.' Sir Robin countered that it was part of his job to push her but the prime minister retorted: 'Yes indeed. It's part of my job to stop you.'   (*The Independent*, 08.08.2000)

Political interviews, then, provide an opportunity for observing the interactional discursive resources that are mobilised by participants of comparable institutional status. This contrasts with the relatively marked asymmetrical status of the participants in the previous two chapters, and correspondingly in the types of discursive strategies deployed by both interviewer and interviewee in their construction of collaborative and conflicting meanings.

NOTES

1. Some of these extracts are taken from a collection of TV broadcasts in Britain recorded during the pre-general election period in May 1987, where one of the main issues in the labour party's campaign was unilateral nuclear disarmament. The consequences and implications of this policy were much discussed in the media during the election campaign (see for instance Garton, Tolson and Montgomery, 1991), some of the interviews also featured American politicians giving their views on the different policies and the possible consequences of a labour victory on the relationship between Britain and the United States.
2. For a discussion of different types of interruption as 'violative' or not, depending on where the onset of overlap occurs, and how it is received by the interruptee, see Hutchby (1992).
3. Cf. also Clayman's (1989) work on interview closings.
4. The term '*overhearing* audience' is something of a misnomer in such contexts. Ratified but indirect recipients of the talk is perhaps a more accurate description of such participants in the talk event.
5. The 'Alliance' was at the time a political grouping in Britain made up of the Liberal Party, led by David Steel, and the Social Democrats, led by Sir David Owen. It was formed out

of the two smaller political parties to produce a stronger third opposition to the Labour and Conservative parties in the 1987 general election.

6. Greatbach (1986) argues that the most successful of these strategies are what he terms pre- and post-answer agenda shifts, which enable interviewees to be heard as answering the question, while at the same time introducing their own topic into the talk. The example below is of an explicitly marked post-answer shift, where interviewee Roy Hattersley moves on to an alternative topic having already produced an answer to the interviewer's question:

(P: 28.9.81: simplified)

```
RH:  → And let me say say something about the next year
        because that was your original question..hhh I think
        Tony Benn would be personally extremely foo:lish
        to sta:nd for the deputy leadership again? [---]
```

(Greatbach, 1986: 444)

7. But see Hutchby's (1997) analysis of a sequence from the TV programme 'Question Time' where one panelist (Michael Heseltine) is aligned against collaboratively by the interviewer and two other panel members, who produce a series of inferential clarifications of what might constitute 'fundamental issues which divide the party'. This results in applause and laughter from the audience at the flouting of Heseltine's point. The third turn receipt position is thus clearly a potentially powerful one for whoever can get access to it, but is of course structurally unavailable to the immediately prior speaker.

8. One of the most well-known walk-outs was by former conservative defence secretary John Nott during an interview with Sir Robin Day just after the Falklands War, when Day suggested that he was a 'here today, gone tomorrow' politician.

9. Jeremy Paxman's guests on this occasion were Henry Kissinger, Geoffrey Robertson QC and Frances Stoner Saunders.

10. This article was published the day after Robin Day's death in August 2000.

6

PARTICIPATION AND CONTROL: THE ORGANISATION OF CLASSROOM DISCUSSION TALK

In the previous three chapters I have been considering contexts for talk where speaker status and identity are institutionally inscribed. In police interviews, radio phone-ins and news or political interviews, I have argued that the rights of access to particular types of discursive identities, such as questioner or formulator, are asymmetrically distributed, and can be constrained both by the structural organisation of the talk and by speakers' relative institutional status. In this final chapter I want to examine another context for interaction, which has long been regarded as inherently asymmetrical, talk in the classroom. First I discuss some of the research which has been centrally concerned with classroom discourse and the power relations that are claimed to hold within it, then I look in more detail at the participation structure of one particular form of classroom interaction, the class discussion.

Edwards and Westgate (1992) have noted that the following features are generally characteristic of 'orderly' classrooms:

> the teacher takes turns at will, allocates turns to others, determines topics, interrupts and reallocates turns judged to be irrelevant to those topics, and provides a running commentary on what is being said and meant. (1992: 46)

In other words, the organisation of classroom interaction is based on a system of unequal distribution of communicative rights and obligations between teachers and pupils.

Since John Sinclair and Malcolm Coulthard's early study (1975) of the use of language in the classroom,[1] analyses of classroom discourse have tended to describe teacher/pupil talk in terms of it being teacher dominated, or teacher led. Sinclair and Coulthard themselves describe the role of the teacher as essentially one of control:

Inside the classroom the single speaker is in control of the many – he[sic] decides who will talk, what they will talk about and also acts as residual speaker, the person who is seen as responsible for dealing with silence.   (1975: 115)

Subsequent studies have built on the exchange model of initiation/response/ follow-up (IRF) to make claims about the kind of actions teachers typically engage in within the classroom, for example 'teachers ask a lot of questions; they often *initiate* discourse topics and they attempt to control the content of classwork by a variety of discourse strategies such as *feedback*' (Fisher, 1993: 239).

THE TEACHING 'EXCHANGE'

One key finding which holds across studies taking very different analytical approaches to the study of classroom talk is that teachers often use a particular form of questioning in the classroom which has been identified as a typical three-part teaching 'exchange'. This form of questioning differs from other kinds of information-seeking questions where the questioner does not know the answer. In a classroom context, teachers clearly do know the answer to many of the questions they ask, and they use these display questions to check what it is that the pupils know. The first part of the exchange involves teachers asking pupils questions which require them to display, in the second part, their response turn, that they know the answer. Pupils' answers are then subject to evaluation in the third part of the exchange, the teacher's 'follow-up' turn. An example of a display question and answer sequence is as follows:

```
T: What's the name of this cutter?
   Hands up.
   ((hand goes up))
   Janet
J: Hacksaw
T: The hacksaw. And I'll put that one there.
```
(Sinclair and Coulthard, 1975: 51)

Here, the teacher elicits a piece of information from the class and invites pupils to bid for the next answering turn by putting up their hands. He selects Janet, whose answer he then accepts and evaluates as an appropriate one simply by repeating it. It is this type of sequence that Sinclair and Coulthard identify as one of the basic teaching exchanges, where each of the three components of the IRF model (initiation/response/follow-up) is realised.

Sinclair and Coulthard also point out that some kind of feedback following a pupil's answering turn is essential in order for them to know whether or not their answer was the right one. If this feedback is witheld, its absence then becomes conditionally relevant; in other words pupils will impute some meaning to that absence, generally that their answer was wrong or inappropriate in some way.[2] It has also been suggested that the prevalence of this kind of exchange in classroom discourse results in pupils frequently being more engaged in developing skills of working out what it is that teachers want to hear, than they are in meaningful learning (Wells and Montgomery, 1981; Fisher, 1993).

Alexander McHoul's (1978) conversation-analytic study of interaction in a US high school classroom describes a similar questioning format. He also found that the management of turns at talk in this context produces what he calls an 'utterance triad' (1978: 191). The triad consists of the following type of turn sequences:

McHoul (5B7-003/H: 120–3)

```
T:     What didju call these
       (1.0) [[indicates on screen]]
( ):   @((whispers)) Sand dunes
       (2.9)
B:     Sa::nd dunes @( )
T:     Sa:::nd dunes alright any other sensible name for it
```

Here we can see the same kind of pattern as the one identified by Sinclair and Coulthard. The teacher elicits some information from the class, and, after some whispering, gets a response from 'B'. The teacher acknowledges that response (again as a repetition of the pupil's answer), puts it on hold ('alright') then requests another possibly more appropriate response.

In his analysis, McHoul identifies some key differences between the rules for conversational turn taking and the rules for the more formal type of interaction that constitutes classroom discourse. First of all, in formal classroom talk the potential for longer gaps between speaker turns is much greater than in ordinary conversation. The pause of almost three seconds between the teacher's questioning turn and a pupil's offered answer in the above extract is an illustration of this. If a teacher has selected a student as next speaker, it is up to the teacher to determine how long that student may have to answer that question, and up to the teacher to decide when and if the answer is sufficient (McHoul, 1978: 190). This results in what he calls 'time out' betweeen turns where students are given the space to produce an answer with no risk of someone else taking their turn.

Second, the potential for overlap is minimised since the teacher selects the next speaker, so there should be less competition for the floor at possible transition points between speakers. McHoul also notes that the one-at-a-time rule in conversation has the added advantage in the context of classsroom interaction of avoiding the possibility of twenty or more speakers at a time. When overlap does occur, teachers re-establish the one-speaker-at-a-time pattern both by explicitly designating a single speaker, and by explicit invocation of the 'rule'. The next extract illustrates an occasion when the rule is breached and most of the class are talking at once. Here is how the teacher repairs this particular outbreak of simultaneous talk.

McHoul (5B5-040: IS-I8S)

```
Class: [((reading out randomly from lists, making up candidate
       [activities.
       [Most of the class are talking at once))
T:     [so there's
       [(4.0)
```

```
T:       [up to around ten is there? Ten diff'rent - sorts of
         [( )
Class:   [((continues to read from lists etc))
B:       [(more)
C:       [(yes)
D:       [(more than that)
-        [-
-        [-
-        [-
T:       Yes [[looks at E]] [[raises both arms diagonally and
         presents palms and outstretched fingers to the class]]
         wait a minute one at a time
E:       On the board you need air conditioning because - during
         December until April it's the a- the air conditioning
         makes ( )
```

The teacher restores the one-at-a-time rule by first designating E as next speaker, at which point the simultaneous talk stops. They then go on to invoke the rule as a reminder, but only once the audience for that reminder has been re-established. McHoul also notes that the teacher's use of gesture as well as the minimal utterance 'yes' enables them to select the next speaker without also contributing to the ongoing simultaneous talk (1978: 199).

The third main difference between conversational interaction and classroom talk identified by McHoul is that the permutability of turn taking is minimised (1978: 189). In other words, the pre-allocation of turns was overwhelmingly 'teacher–student–teacher–student', and deviations from this pattern are subject to repair. He also notes that, in his data, most of the talking was done by the teacher, and in predominantly monologic form, so that the very possibility for speakers to take equal turns was reduced. Furthermore, teachers are able to extend their turns without fear of another participant self selecting at a completion point, and, in view of this, are able to break up their talk with long intra-turn pauses.

The speech exchange system in the kind of classroom talk McHoul describes produces an institutional formality because there is a high degree of pre-allocation of turn types, and an asymmetrical distribution of those turns between participants. The participation rights and obligations of teachers and pupils in classroom interaction are clearly differentiated, he suggests, in that 'the locally managed component is largely the domain of teachers, student participation rights being limited to the choice between continuing or selecting the teacher as next speaker' (1978: 211). The teacher instigates topics, asks questions, decides what counts as a sufficient answer, determines how long students get to produce one and comments on whether it is adequate or not, thus occupying the role of director of the talk. On the other hand, these rights are countered by an obligation on the teacher's part to provide students with an indication of whether they have produced an adequate answer or not.

Despite the very different theoretical approaches that these two studies adopt in their account of classroom talk, the former predicated on a structural linguistic model, and the latter on the situated, sequential model of conversation analysis, there are some clear parallels which emerge between their findings. The role of the teacher in both sets of data is described as either directive or controlling. Teachers engage in similar kinds of discursive actions (topic initiation, eliciting, selecting next speakers) and the talk typically follows a three-part sequence of teacher initiation, pupil response and teacher comment or feedback. Similarly, the expectation on the part of the pupils that the teacher's role is to provide that feedback is also noted by both McHoul and Sinclair and Coulthard. McHoul's analysis highlights the particular institutional nature of classroom talk, in terms of the formal organisation of turns at talk, and the asymmetrical allocation of turn types and participation rights in that context. The type of teaching sequence analysed in both studies has an in-built differential in participant status: one participant who 'knows' the answer evaluates the knowledge, or lack of it, of all the others. In this situation, the discourse roles of elicitor and evaluator are institutionally occupied by the teacher; those of 'displayer' and 'evaluatee' are occupied by the pupils.[3]

INSTRUCTIONAL TALK AS 'ASYMMETRICAL'

The talk that is produced through this particular distribution of turn types and relative participant status is recognisably instructional (Drew, 1981). Instructional talk can also take place between adults and children at home, as well as between teachers and pupils in schools. The main difference between the two contexts is the way that parents correct children in the third 'feedback' turn compared to teacher corrections of pupils. The example below shows a mother correcting her child in the course of some instructional talk:

```
M: now what number's that
   ((pointing to position of hands on clock))
R: Number two
M: No it's not
M: What is it
M: Its a one and a nought
```

(BLDP: Extract A, taken from Drew, 1981)

The mother uses a very direct and unmitigated contradiction 'no it's not' in response to her child's offer of an answer; teachers, however, use other kinds of less-direct strategies to elicit a 'better' answer from pupils, as we have seen in the extract from McHoul's data above, 'sa::nd dunes alright any other sensible name for it'. Another example of parent/child interaction which demonstrates the same point, taken from a conversation about the day's activities between two parents and their two year old child during supper.[4] The mother is asking the child about his day:

```
M: you went to the ducks
C: yes
M: and where do the ducks live
C: in an an in a swimming pool
M: in the swimming pool
C: yes
M: rubbish
```

M's question 'and where do the ducks live' is designed to elicit already known information from the child. Her treatment of C's answer echoes the directness of the mother in the previous example, 'no it's not'. This type of bald 'on record' contradiction (Brown and Levinson, 1987) is a dispreferred option for teachers, despite their apparently more powerful status as participants within the classroom, whereas in parent–child interaction the force of a direct contradiction of the child's answer, 'rubbish', is mitigated in this context by the close family relationship between the participants.

In much of the research into specifically instructional discourse in the classroom, there is a pervasive assumption that teachers occupy a role of authority and power. This authority is inherent in the nature of most educational institutions, structured by the demands of the curriculum, and in the 'learning' agenda.[5] The teacher necessarily is (or at least is supposed to be) in control of what happens in the classroom. This assumption is made explicit in Fisher's (1993) observation that 'classroom discourse research also suggests that many teachers control the content and direction of the discourse by asking questions and by reformulating the answers that pupils give' (1993: 421). It also underpins Chouliaraki's (1996) claim that teachers use 'progressivist' pedagogic practices in order to regulate and control pupils. In training them to adopt 'good habits' in the classroom (for example, how to listen properly, how to write), she suggests that this focus on *how* something should be done, rather than *why*, while it may develop the procedural competence of pupils, operates covertly to maintain the established institutional order. Even in the conversation-analytic approach taken by McHoul (1978), an asymmetrical distribution of power in classroom interaction is assumed in his discussion of the limited participation 'rights' of students.

However, the notion that power is a resource that is 'owned' by teachers and not by pupils is very much open to question. Alison Jones (1989) found in her study of classroom practice in a New Zealand secondary school that pupils can also be well aware that what *they* do shapes the actions of the teacher:

She asks me to ask questions. I never ask questions. I just keep quiet and I always say, 'What?' when she asks me questions so she has to ask them twice.   (1989: 24)

This student's comment shows that she is well aware of the resources available to her through which she can effectively resist the teacher's agenda, and that resistance is produced through the use of particular discursive strategies. In a classroom context, then, we may need to look at power less as something clearly owned by teachers, and more as a state of affairs brought about by a relationship which is continuously under negotiation between all participants.

In a recent ethnographic study of how power relations worked in three elementary school classrooms, Mary Phillips Manke (1997) draws on Foucault's theoretical metaphor of power as a net or web, where power is not the property of any individual, but something which is constantly being exercised, experienced and resisted by all social actors (see my discussion of power in chapter 1). Taking the view that power relations are jointly constructed between teachers and pupils, Manke explores the resources used by all participants within the practice of classroom interaction.

She is particularly interested in issues such as how classroom time and space are organised, how classroom knowledge gets defined, what kind of discursive strategies of indirectness and politeness are used in teacher/student interaction and how students resist teachers' agendas. Manke found that teachers were drawing upon discursive resources such as politeness markers, the use of inclusive 'we' to refer to the class, general statements of rules and principles rather than individual reprimands and frequent use of indirect directives to pupils, for example, 'it's really better if desks are tidy' (p. 78). She argues that these resources do not just serve to reduce the asymmetry of social distance between teachers and pupils and to strengthen pupils' self-esteem, rather she suggests that teachers use them because they are constantly aware of the level of collusion which it is necessary to establish between them and their pupils for the teaching agenda to operate successfully.[6] The use of these discursive strategies may also help to avoid confrontation with pupils, and the possible loss of control over the classroom environment which might ensue.

Manke's study of the construction of power relations in these three elementary school classes provides some useful insights into what is going on for both teachers and children within the context of talk in the classroom. For example, she describes how '[c]onsistently, students in the three classrooms (with or without their teacher's encouragement) were seen making connections between what was presented as classroom knowledge and what they knew from other experiences' (p. 105). These connections were to do with relating the task at hand either to wider issues in the world or to their own particular agenda. As an illustration of this Manke cites how one boy resisted the teacher's instructions to carry out a research project by saying: 'I already know a lot about Robin Hood in my head' (p. 104). His agenda was to write what he knew, rather than comply with the teacher's agenda of preparing a research topic.

Another way in which children can resist the agenda of the teacher is to simulate misunderstandings of instructions, as we saw with the older pupil quoted from Jones' study above. An example from Manke's data is the following exchange at the start of a routine spelling test in fifth grade:

```
Marlon:          What unit?
Ms Bridgestone:  Stadium
Marlon:          No what unit
Ms Bridgestone:  Twenty-five
LaToya:          You can see it on the board
```

(Manke, 1997: 108)

In this extract, Marlon persists in asking for clarification to such an extent that another pupil points out that the answer is clearly visible to him. As Manke observes, one outcome of these kinds of 'misunderstandings' is the momentary disruption of established routine classroom activities, such as spelling tests. Clearly unwarranted clarification requests are therefore another discursive strategy that pupils can deploy to resist the teacher's agenda.

Manke's study suggests that, in order to locate and understand power relations in the classroom, we need to pay close attention to the interactional and discursive resources that all the members of the classroom exploit in order to pursue their respective, and sometimes conflicting, agendas. However, although she provides many examples of the participation and talk produced in classroom activities from her video and audio recordings as well as from her own observational notes, her transcripts are not detailed enough to enable a close analysis of what Gene Lerner (1995) calls 'the moment-to-moment (that is, turn-by-turn) opportunities made available for that participation in the course of those activities' (p. 112). Indeed, Manke particularly mentions the various difficulties she encountered in transcribing classroom data that contained the talk of many students rather than the talk of one teacher; it is a complex and 'inevitably incomplete' task (p. 106).

Transcription is particularly complex when the level of formality in classroom interaction is low. The classroom speech exchange system described by McHoul (1978) is based on the 'one-speaker-at-a-time' rule and a high degree of pre-allocated turn types. The distribution of types of turn between teachers and pupils reduces the uncertainty of who speaks next, but this is not necessarily the norm in more progressivist classrooms, where instruction is less teacher centred. It is certain that the transcription of recorded talk in this kind of teaching environment presents a challenge to any analyst who wants to describe the particular nature and organisational dynamics of multi-party classroom interaction. Even when the activity observed is a relatively structured one, such as a discussion based on whole class participation where the 'one-at-a-time' rule *is* explicitly invoked, there are many moments where more than one person talks at a time. There is often a great deal being accomplished during those moments, in and around what Edwards and Westgate (1992) refer to as 'the edges of the official channels' for participation, which is very difficult to capture in a transcript. They too point out that teacher-directed talk is much more easily accessible to analysts: 'it may be that the pervasiveness of closely teacher-directed forms of classroom talk has been unwittingly exaggerated by researchers because these are the forms which are easiest, or least difficult, to record and interpret' (p. 44).

However complex and inevitably partial the task of transcribing such talk may be, in the following analysis of classroom discussion data I show that what we can observe about the participation frameworks in the talk, by paying attention to 'the edges' as well as to the more obviously central exchanges in such contexts, can be well worth the effort involved.

THE DISCUSSION AS A CLASSROOM ACTIVITY TYPE

In classroom discussions, where pupils are given the opportunity to talk about their own experiences and those of other people, there may be a temporary relaxation of the authoritative role of the teacher. However, discussion talk as an activity is still organised quite formally. Edwards and Westgate (1992) note the basic interactional groundrules for a discussion are 'don't hog the floor, don't interrupt, listen to others and make some reference to what they have said' (p. 53). But even during this kind of talk, as research into classroom discourse has indicated, there is still a tendency for teacher-directed forms of interaction to predominate. Although teachers may recognise the positive benefits to children's learning in having opportunities to talk in the classroom, Edwards and Westgate point out that one consequence of backlash from traditionalists who advocate a return to 'whole class teaching' is in fact the restriction of that space. To challenge the traditional primacy of teacher-directed talk in the classroom is to redistribute powerful resources to children, and this redistribution can result in a potential loss of control for teachers. With these issues in mind, I now want to turn to some classroom data in order to look at what can be said about the resources for managing the talk during a discussion, ostensibly a controlled space for children to talk, and how the resources are distributed between teacher and pupils.

DISCUSSIONS IN A YEAR SIX CLASSROOM

The data I focus on here are taken from a British primary school year six classroom of 10–11 year olds. The talk is not instructional in the sense of the examples discussed earlier, in that the teacher is not in the position of owning some 'knowledge' to be transmitted to pupils. Rather, it is an activity designed to get the children to formulate and express their opinions on a particular issue and to participate in an orderly discussion of that issue. Listening to what others have to say is also an important aspect of this activity. Several questions then arise about the organisation of this kind of talk. How are turn types distributed and turns at talk allocated in this situation? How do teachers get children talking about their opinions, and how do they get them to stop? Do any changes emerge in the course of this kind of activity in relation to the participation roles and rights of the children and teacher, and, finally, how is this talk constructed and displayed as a particular orderly form of institutional discourse? I will deal with these questions in turn, but, first, here is a brief description of the data on which I base my analysis.

The class discussion data presented in this chapter are selected from a larger corpus of different settings for talk in an upper primary classroom in a London school. The pupils are in their last year of primary education (year six). Discussions were held regularly as part of the learning activities in this class, and these sessions were recorded by the class (with no researcher present) at various points throughout the year. The recorded discussions usually start with an introductory clarifying utterance which sets the scene for what is to follow, for example:

```
Do we know what we're talking about?
Today we're going to be talking about our secondary school.
This discussion's about ...
```

The discussion involves the whole class. The talk takes place in an area of the classroom known as the 'carpet', where most of the whole class teaching takes place, with the children all sitting close together on the floor and the teacher sitting on a low chair. The topics for discussion are generated by current issues in the news (for example, the debate about a football club manager's religious beliefs) or are linked to children's current life experiences (getting on with people, going on a school journey, stealing from other children, taking entrance tests for secondary schools). The discussions follow a similar structural framework and usually last for up to twenty minutes of class time. Once the topic has been introduced quite formally by one of the pupils (as in the examples above), the talk moves through repeated sequences of mainly one-speaker-at-a-time talk.

HOW ARE TURN TYPES DISTRIBUTED AND TURNS AT TALK ALLOCATED?

Pupils take quite long extended turns in which they can do a variety of things, depending on the nature of the topic: they give opinions, describe their feelings, tell stories, hypothesise about situations, and more. Access to these turns is regulated by the teacher, who designates next speakers either by name or occasionally through some non-verbal signal in response to a bid for the floor:

```
Michael
(huh) Alex
go on Benj
right shh Rosie.
```

The teacher also most frequently occupies the position of primary recipient of the current speaker's talk; that is, she takes the third 'receipt' turn in the sequence, in which she acknowledges the end of the current speaker's contribution and selects the next speaker:

```
okay thank you er Sophie
right (.) erm Saskia
ok Tom
```

This initial description of how the turn types are distributed in order to formally organise the discussion as a classroom event is however a deceptively simplified one, and the one-at-a-time structure of the talk I have just invoked is perhaps misleading. The 'one-at-a-time' format, where one participant is given access to an extended turn at talk while the others listen, tends to hold initially at least for the first few speakers. But as the discussion gains momentum, the talk is transformed into something much more complex as other pupils begin to contribute to the talk. In the next section I want to examine in much more detail what can occur in the course of a discussion, and, particularly, what is the role of the other pupils in constructing it as a multi-party event.

The following extracts from the data illustrate these different stages of participation in the talk. The first is an example of how things typically go at the beginning of a discussion. The topic is 'going to secondary school'. This extract shows the teacher assessing a prior contribution, selecting the next speaker, then, recursively, assessing that contribution and selecting the next one.

Secondary School Segment 4

```
 1. Teacher: got into (xxx). what a relief
 2.            (.) Emma
 3. Emma:     well um I was happy that I got into (xxx)
 4.           cos um (.) lots of people applied to that school
 5.           but um (.) I'm going to be sad when I leave
 6.           primary school cos I'm gonna (.) leave (.)
 7.           most of my friends (.) which are here
 8.           and quite a (lot'v) people gonna go like that
 9.           if they're not going to the same school
10.           [(as their friends)           ]
11. Teacher: [yeah I think you're right]
12.           (.) Ben
```

This is a neatly bound sequence which occurs three minutes into the discussion. The participation framework is also quite clearly delineated in the distribution of turn-types. The teacher's alignment as primary recipient of the pupils' talk is evident in her acknowledgement of their contributions, as in 'what a relief' (line 1). As soon as Emma reaches a likely completion point (line 10), the teacher again takes the next turn with an assessment, 'yeah I think you're right'. Her role as floor allocator is also clearly evident in this extract; in lines 2 and 12, after an assessment token, there is a slight pause, then she selects the next speaker, nominating 'Emma' then 'Ben'. The selected speaker's role is to produce an opinion when she is given the floor, 'well um I was happy that I got into (. . .)', while the teacher's main role is to assess that contributed opinion. Through this assessment turn she closes the floor to the current speaker and opens it up for the next one. The talk is orderly in the sense that only one pupil talks at a time, the talk is both teacher elicited and teacher evaluated, and the same sequential pattern which occurs here can be identified early on in the other discussions in the corpus.

The next extract, on the topic of what they would do if they saw someone from their class stealing another pupil's money, occurs just under two minutes into the talk and shows the same participation structure:

Stealing Money Segment 6

```
 1. Teacher: good point (xxx) ri:ght
 2.            (.) Jack
 3. Jack:     w- what I'd do is I'd go up to them
 4.           and I'd give them a certain amount of time (.)
 5.           before I told the teacher (.)
 6.           and if they didn't give it back in that time (.)
 7.           you can tell the teacher
 8.           and then you can just say if they (.) start
 9.           bullying you you can just say oh I warned you.
10. Teacher: right ↑right↓
11.           Rosie
```

However, as the discussion progresses, the clearly bound three-part structure of these sequences is much less in evidence. Pupils begin to display a much more active participant role as recipients of each others' talk by also taking up assessment positions once an opinion has been produced. In the following extract, after the end of Rosie's turn, which is a strongly stated view with a hearably complete ending, the teacher's 'mmm' (line 11) is followed by other candidate assessment turns:

Glen Hoddle Segment 7

```
 8. Rosie:    but (.) well (.) frankly I think he should (.)
 9.           just keep his mouth shut unless
10.           he's talking about football
11. Teacher: mmm=
12. ?:        =yeah=
13. ?:        =um=
14. ?:        =but
15. Teacher: (ok Tom)
```

Here it is not just the teacher who says 'mmm' once Rosie has finished, but there are three further receipt tokens in turns taken in rapid succession by three different pupils at lines 12, 13 and 14. The final 'but' indicates a probable disagreement with her position. However the important observation here is that there are clearly a number of candidates aligning themselves as potential next speaker.

Further evidence that pupils position themselves as legitimate potential occupiers of the immediate next turn, once an opinion has been produced, can also be found in the next extract, even if they do not actually manage to hold on to the floor:

Glen Hoddle Segment 6

```
13. Saskia   and (.) um (1.0) but (.) I- I don't see why
14.          (0.9) it was such a problem (.) that he said that
15.          cos it's just what he believes
16.          I don't think [he said it to offend anybody]
17. Boy?:                  [(xxx) he said that           ]
18. Teacher: right
19. Saskia:  that's just what he believes=
20. Tom:     =um well (.) one he said
21. Girl?:   °Rosie°
22. Teacher: right then (hold on)
```

In line 17 a pupil self selects as next speaker in overlap with the end of Saskia's turn before the teacher's assessment token 'right'. In line 20, another boy (Tom) has a response ready and organised into points, as his placing of a marked stress on 'one' seems to indicate that he has more than one thing to say to contest her position. In line 21, though, another pupil whispers 'Rosie', possibly proposing her as a candidate next speaker. The teacher appears to accept this nomination, as Rosie is selected as next speaker and Tom has to wait for the next teacher allocated speaker slot before he can make his points.

So, as the discussion moves on, pupils begin to do much more than just listen while one speaker after another takes their extended turn at contributing an opinion. Within the basic participation framework I described earlier of 'one-person-at-a-time' talk, with that person selected by the teacher, there is a wealth of other activity taking place within the space of one pupil's occupancy of the floor. In spite of the fact that there are so many of them, the pupils begin to display their 'active listenership' through contributing receipt comments, assessments and disagreements, but without disrupting the orderliness of the event.

SHIFTING PARTICIPANT RIGHTS AND ROLES

In the next extract, from nearly nineteen minutes into the secondary school discussion, the participation framework has changed considerably. As designated speaker, Alex is telling a story about what happened when he went to take the entrance test for one of the local secondary schools:

Secondary school Segment 19, 18:59

```
 1. Teacher:  um Alex
 2. Alex:     um (0.6) well (.) like (.) when I went to (xxx)[7]
 3.           it was like >really cool cos like< (.)
 4.           I had Sam on one side of me and Pip was next doing-
 5.           playing with his thermometer pen
 6.           and [um
 7. ?:            [huhhuh]h[m
 8. ?:            [hmhm  ] [hm=
 9. ?:        =huh
10. Boy:      (I remember) his ther<u>mo</u>meter [  pen      (xxx)  ]
11. Alex:                              [and Jack was (.)]
12.           and like (.)Jack was at the front
```

The opening two turns of this sequence are typical in that they consist of the teacher's nomination of Alex as next speaker, and Alex's take up of the floor. He starts his account of the experience by saying how it was 'cool' because his friends were close around him. Then he mentions Pip's 'thermometer pen' (line 5). At this point several pupils laugh in response, one even says 'I remember his thermometer pen', before Alex picks up his story again in line 11. This is clearly talk designed for the other members of the class, not just for the teacher. Alex is constructing his story here as one which contains familiar characters doing familiar things, and the other pupils actively produce displays of their recipiency and alignment to the way Alex is building his story for them. Their laughter, and one pupil's explicit acknowledgement of remembering 'the thermometer pen', at the same time show Alex that his audience is attentively with him at this stage.

Another moment during this story which triggers pupils' laughter is a further mention of Pip and his pen:

```
19. Alex:    I turned round and looked at Pip (.)
20.          and Pip was like making a seesaw with the
21.          thermometer pen and I was thinking
22.          [(0.8) I was thinking God=
23. ?:       [↑huhhuh
```

```
24. Alex:     =Pip's already fi- finished and stuff and
25.            then um [Sam
26. Boy:              [huh
27. Alex:     Sam was just sittin' there twiddling his thumbs
28.           and stuff [and I was ]
29. ?:                  [  huhuh  ]
30. Alex:     and I was trying to think of like
31.           the rest of the (.) answers and stuff (.)
32.           and um and it was it was quite scary actually (0.5)
33. Teacher: [it is
```

Alex's amusing description of how he can see that his friends in the test have finished when he has not, gets appropriate responses of laughter from the others in the class. But the laughter (lines 26 and 29) also occcurs in response to Alex's growing unease about the situation, which he foregrounds in a rhetorically structured way (lines 22 through to 31). The three utterances which lead up to his evaluation of the event as 'quite scary' are syntactically similar:

```
Pip's already finished and stuff
Sam was just sittin' there twiddling his thumbs and stuff
I was trying to think of like the rest of the answers and stuff
```

This is also a three part list sequence where the last item in the list contrasts with the first two: Alex's trouble v. Pip and Sam's apparent ease with the test. After the first two there is a laughter token from someone in the class, but once he gets to his own position, and gives a story evaluation (line 32), the teacher takes the next turn with an affiliative response, 'it is'. This is a clear transition point, a moment when Alex is heard to have given a complete opinion, and a new speaker could be nominated. However, he has more to tell. The next part of his story, where it turns out that he did in fact fail to get in to this school, is a highly collaborative sequence. Here is the final episode of his story:

```
32.           and um and it was it was quite scary actually (0.5)
33. Teacher: [it is
34. Alex:    [and then um
35. Boy:     dum dum du[m dum
36. Alex:              [°and then°
37.          and then and then I had and then um (0.6)
38.          I got the letter and >I thought it was very< rude
39.          because they said said
40.          sorry you haven't got into (xxx) (0.5)
41.          [like
42. Boy:     [(xxx)?
43. Alex:    [um
44. Boy:     [>I thought you said< [(xxx)
45. Alex:                         [(xxx) but like this
46.          and I thought I thought they could have said a bit
47.          more but like they didn't
48. ?:       sorry [you haven't got in
49. Alex:          [and
```

```
50. ?:        sorry
51. ?:        shame
52. ?:        (I remember having the)
53. ?:        shame [(              )
54. Alex:          [and then
55. Teacher?:      [yeah
56. ?:        (                  )
57. Alex:     and then [um also] I um (.) I °I I I I°
58. ?:        I I I:
59. Teacher:  (I'll) come back ok
60. Alex:     yeah
61. ?:        I I ↑I
62. Teacher:  um
63. ?:        I I I
64. ?:        >°huhuh°<
65. Teacher:  Tasha?
```

After Alex's evaluation of his experience as 'scary' there is a slight pause, but he continues, in overlap with the teacher who has self selected at that moment to take a receipt and, as we have seen, potentially closing turn. With his continuing 'and then' Alex makes it clear that he wants more space to tell the rest of his story, and the dramatic turn is picked up by another pupil in line 35 who goes 'dum dum dum dum'. This is conventionally recognised as a rhythmical sound beat to signal a 'scary moment' when something dramatic is about to happen. Alex builds this up by repeating 'and then' several times (lines 36 and 37), and then moves on to the next event: the arrival of the letter telling him that he hasn't got in to the school.

```
38. Alex: I got the letter and >I thought it was very< rude
39.       because they said said
40.       sorry you haven't got into (xxx) (0.5)
41.       [like
42. Boy:  [(xxx)?
43. Alex: [um
44. Boy:  [>I thought you said< [(xxx)
45. Alex:                       [(xxx) but like this
```

At this point he gets the name of the school wrong. This error is the subject of some repair work in the next turn when another boy produces a repair initiator, the name of the school '(xxx)?' (line 42) and another correction, 'I thought you said (xxx)' (line 44), which Alex accepts. Once this problem has been sorted out, the 'rude' tone of the letter becomes topicalised in an interesting way by several members of the class:

```
45. Alex:                       [(xxx) but like this
46.       and I thought I thought they could have said a bit
47.       more but like they didn't
48. ?:    sorry [you haven't got in
49. Alex:       [and
50. ?:    sorry
51. ?:    shame
52. ?:    (I remember having the)
```

```
53. ?:          shame [(                    )
54. Alex:             [and then
55. Teacher?:         [yeah
56. ?:          (                    )
57. Alex:       and then [um also] I um (.) I °I I I I°
58. ?:          I I I:
59. Teacher:    (I'll) come back ok
```

Alex's comment that 'they could have said a bit more' (line 46) gets taken up by another pupil in line 48. One pupil starts by animating the voice of the letter (Goffman, 1981), then others take up the same footing with their contributions of 'sorry' and 'shame' over the next four turns. It sounds as if another pupil (line 52) might also be offering some solidarity with Alex's experience by referring to receiving a similar letter: 'I remember having the'. Finally (line 57), Alex runs into trouble – his attempt at hanging on to the floor 'I- I- I-' is echoed by some others and it is at that point that the teacher intervenes to close down Alex's turn. The way she does this, by intimating that he will get another chance to talk, 'I'll come back ok', is also an example of her attention to the delicacy of his story. It is a story of a failure, but it is told with some considerable rhetorical skill and humour, and it produces a high level of collaborative support in contributions from his peer co-participants.

What we can see in this sequence therefore is very different from the earlier extract in several ways. First, this is narrative discourse, rather than opinion giving. Oral narratives are contextually sensitive, and are designed for specific recipients (Sacks, 1978; Schiffrin, 1984). The other members of the class display a clear orientation to their role as primary recipients of Alex's story by producing receipt tokens of laughter and appropriate collaborative comments, whereas the primary recipient of Emma's opinion early in the discussion is the teacher. Second, when Alex gets a detail wrong, the error is picked up in the next turn by another pupil, and the business of the school name and its accuracy is dealt with entirely and successfully between the two boys. Pupils in this context, then, self select to do repair work, without teacher sanction. This is a role that in instructional talk is more likely to be taken by a teacher rather than a peer. Third, the active engagement of other participants in co-producing this story (the dramatic moment sound effects, the animation of the letter) results in more than one-speaker-at-a-time talk, without being a violation of the one-at-a-time rule that is supposed to hold in more formal occasions for talk in the classroom. Rather than consider this talk as on the edge, and extraneous to the principal floor, I would argue that it is a highly ordered and cohesive display of collaborative talk. In this extract participants are not rigidly divided into roles of speaker and listeners, but shift in and out of different kinds of participatory footings in relation to the talk of the speaker who officially 'owns' the floor at that moment, for the space of their teacher-designated extended turn.

REGULATING THE TALK

So far I have looked at the pattern of the talk in terms of the different participant roles available to speakers, and how they get taken up. I have suggested that discussion talk in this classroom becomes a highly collaborative activity in which the pupils attend closely to each others' contributions and build on the themes that emerge in the course of the talk. The teacher's primary role is managing the boundary transitions between one designated speaker and another, once the current speaker's extended turn is hearable as complete, but not to manage transitions between speakers within the space of that turn as long as speakers' contributions are relevant and therefore ratified, that is they are not treated as sanctionable talk.

There are of course points in the discussion where too many people are talking at once for any one speaker to be heard, particularly towards the end of the activity when the initial one-at-a-time framework has evolved into a much more multi-participation event. At these points, the teacher takes up a more overtly regulative role, usually by going: 'shhh'. The following extract is one such instance when the discussion is in danger of becoming untenable:

Glen Hoddle Segment 21

```
 1. ?:       =[they did=
 2. ?:       =[yeah but=
 3. boy?:    =[but they do (.) [they do he's just more skilled   ]
 4. ?:                          [yeah I know but Mar-Michael Owen]
 5. boy?:    (Michael Owen)
 6. ?:       so (he wasn't even (xxx)=
 7. boy?:                           =huh huh=
 8. boy?:                                   =hah hah
 9. boys:    =((joint laughter---[---])                         ]
10. Sophie:                      [(and Michael Owen)]=
11. Sophie:  =[(was having] (xxx)(all the fame)=
12. ?:        [   sshhh  ]
13. boy?:                     [Michael Jamieson]
14. Sophie:  =[(without the [(xxx)              ]
15. ?:                      [shhh              ]
16. Teacher: sorry I can't hear start again Sophie
17. Sophie:  erm Michael Owen was having all the um
18.          all the fame so I (.) maybe he's just doing it
19.          so (.) you know other people could
```

As the increased stretches of overlapping talk in the transcript indicate, the interaction becomes more complex here as another parallel floor develops between two or three other pupils who are no longer contributing to the discussion, but impeding it. Sophie is still talking during the boys' laughter and comments about the name Michael Owen, and at two points someone, possibly the teacher, goes 'sshh'. The sanction does not occur verbally until the utterance in line 16 'sorry I can't hear start again'. By reallocating the floor to Sophie in this turn, the teacher reinstates her as the current speaker whose talk is to take precedence over the other, parallel floors.

Later in this sequence, once Sophie has finished making her point about Glen Hoddle giving other footballers in the England team a chance, at least three pupils respond in disagreement, which gives rise to the following intervention by the teacher:

```
boys?:    [ (xxx)        ]
Teacher: [sssshhhhh erm]=
boy:                      =England shouted=
Teacher:                              =Siobhan
Siobhan: um I (.) I don't think he should have said that
         but [-.--]
```

The teacher begins her turn by saying 'sshh' but she also places the continuer 'erm' at the end of the turn. Despite this sanction, and the indication that she is about to select the next speaker, one boy makes a final contribution in the series of responses to Sophie's point. The teacher then immediately latches her next turn to this, and nominates the next speaker. In doing so, she again returns the floor to a single speaker who takes up the next turn, and the talk is restored to its earlier format.

In the final stages, one of the other pupils takes on the sanctioning role:

```
Pip: why is he sinning and doing all this
     [bad stuff like publishing]
     [((Laughter---))           ]
     showing [like (his) private letters]
?:           [Joe will you shut↑up↓      ]
```

So it is when the talk is at risk of moving out of being recognisably 'discussion' and becoming something much looser in terms of who is talking and to what purpose, that the sanctions occur, with either the teacher, or as in the above extract, another pupil, taking responsibility for the regulatory move. Interestingly, the pupil uses the unmitigated, indeed aggravated directive form 'Joe will you shut↑up↓' while the teacher uses much less direct strategies in her calls to order. Either she goes 'sshh', or as in segment 21 above, she addresses the designated current speaker, in this case Sophie, thereby indirectly targeting the others who are making the noise. The teacher's use of a nomination to designate next speaker seems a more powerful resource for returning the talk to a more orderly format than the more direct 'sshh'. This strategy is similar to those noticed by Manke (1997), who suggests that teachers use these kind of indirect utterances in order to maintain the necessary level of collusion within the classroom, and avoid risking direct confrontation, rather than to attend to the positive face needs of the pupils.

The teacher also intervenes as a regulator when a contribution is deemed to be inappropriate in some way. In the following extract, the pupil who interrupts at line 17 is sanctioned by the teacher's repeated 'sh' in lines 18 and 20:

Glen Hoddle Segment 8

```
13.            but I don't think [he should have been   ] sacked=
14. ?:                           [(no I don't think so)]
15. ?:         =it's what he believes=
16. Tom?:      =[because uh-
17. ?:         [but this disabled [bloke came running in
18. Teacher:                     [shhh   sh     sh
```

```
19. ?:        an' (.) started a riot]=
20. Teacher:  sh     sh   sh        ]
21. Tom:      =because um (.) I mean (.) it's what (.) what he
22.           thinks (.)he should keep it to himself (.)
```

In contrast to the utterances in lines 14 and 15 which are supporting Tom's point, this turn is both structurally interruptive, in that Tom has not finished giving his reasoning for his point of view, and topically interruptive, in that it attempts to shift the focus away from the issue of whether Glen Hoddle should have been sacked or not to an episode from a TV programme the previous day, which has little bearing on the current ethical topic of the discussion. By sanctioning this kind of disruptive contribution to the discussion the teacher gives Tom the space to finish his argument on a clear completion point, keeping the topic on course and providing a receipt token 'right' before the (non-verbal) designation of the next speaker:

```
21. Tom:      =because um (.) I mean (.) it's what (.) what he
22.           thinks (.) he should keep it to himself (.)
23.           but it's what he thinks
24.           and I don't think he should be sacked (for it)
25. Teacher:  right
```

However, there is very little evidence of this type of disruptive talk in the class discussion corpus I am using here. Most calls to order occur when the 'rules' for participation are not being adhered to and too many pupils are either vying for the next floor occupancy, or talking at once in response to someone's point, or developing parallel floors. Explicit invocation of the 'one-at-a-time' rule is used in 'queueing' utterances such as:

```
hang on one at a time
right hang on
```

and utterances which draw attention to the need for currently produced talk to be both ratified and relevant:

```
Ben have you got something to say
```

As I have shown here, both teacher and pupils engage in regulatory actions, and peer regulation is particularly direct, but it is still only the teacher who regulates access to the floor by designating ratified next speakers.

In these data, there is evidence of a high level of engagement on the part of most participants with the business of producing a discussion as a classroom event. To return to Manke's notion of control in classrooms as 'collusion', it seems that the pupils are not just colluding, but in most cases actively collaborating with the teacher and their peers in the joint accomplishment of talk which constitutes the genre of 'discussion'. I now look in more detail at how this discussion talk is oriented to by the participants as a particular contextualised form of institutional discourse.

CLASSROOM DISCUSSION AS INSTITUTIONAL TALK

The successful production of a discussion depends crucially on the collaboration of most (if not all) of the participants. In other words, a discussion is an activity which can only be jointly accomplished if the ratified participants in the talk display to the others that they agree on, and will hold to, certain discursive roles and appropriate behaviours in those roles. If one participant resists taking up their role, then this causes some momentary trouble as can be seen in the following extract:

Stealing money Segment 20

```
 1. Teacher:  yeah right
 2.           (.)
 3.           Luke
 4. Luke:     mm?
 5. Teacher:  what do you think?
 6. Luke:     I don't know
 7. ?:        nuhuh
 8. Teacher:  you don't [know.
 9. ?:                  [(I'm thinking about it)
10. ?:        wah waah wah waah
11. ?:        °shh°
12. ?:        [(laughter)]
13. ?:        [(xxx)     ]
14. Teacher:  Sam
15. Sam:      well I think it would be like really hard [---]
```

The difference between Luke's take up of his designated speaker turn (line 4), and the way that all the other pupils do it, is striking. If we look at Sam's take up of his turn (line 15), several comparisons immediately become noticeable. First, Luke goes 'mm?' in response to the teacher's nomination of him as next speaker. In all four recorded class discussions in my data, this is the only case where a pupil does this. In the vast majority of cases, pupils display their orientation to their discursive role as opinion givers in that next turn, and what Luke's 'mm?' clearly displays here is his inattention. In contrast, Sam goes 'well I think . . .' which is typical of the way pupils design their next turn when they have just been nominated by the teacher as next speaker.[8] Here are just three such examples from the data, of which there are many more:

```
well what I'd do ...
well it was a stupid thing to say ...
I think it's like really bad ...
```

Second, the teacher makes the question explicit in her next turn: 'what do you think?' In every other case, simply naming the next speaker is sufficient to produce an appropriate response from them in relation to what might be expected in this context. In other words, after the teacher nominates the next pupil to speak, the expectation is that they will take up their position as designated speaker in the next turn, by either producing an opinion or making some other similarly relevant and appropriate contribution (for example, Alex's story above). Luke does neither. Moreover, his answer 'I don't know' produces several reactions from the rest of the class. First of all at line 7 someone laughs slightly, then at lines 9 and 10 more pupils manifest some other reaction to Luke's lack of opinion. Although it is quite difficult to distinguish exactly what is said here, what does seem clear is that in making these noises, they are responding not just to the fact that he doesn't know, but also displaying their awareness of the fact that saying you don't know is not playing the game in this context. In other words, by saying 'I don't know' Luke is resisting taking part in the collective activity at hand. If a substantial majority of the participants resisted like this, the activity as such would break down, and there would be no discussion.

Throughout this classroom discussion data then, there is a clear sense in which not only the teacher but also the pupils are engaged in holding the talk within certain procedural constraints. For example, there is evidence that the pupils are actively participating as attentive listeners to each other's talk, as we have seen in Alex's story above, but also at many other moments during the discussions. There is also clear evidence that the majority of pupils do take up their role as 'opinion producers' when invited to do so by the teacher. They also display their position as recipients of each others' opinions, despite the teacher's tendency to occupy third turn receipt position in the initial stages of the discussions.

In the final part of this chapter I want to discuss one last extract which illustrates the ways in which the participants display their collaboration in jointly producing a discussion as a classroom event, in other words, as institutional discourse. There are many examples of this type of collaborative building of discussion talk in the data, which I do not have the space to show here, but the extract below is representative of many sequences which together constitute the discussions recorded in this classroom. It is taken from the discussion about stealing money:

Stealing money Segment 40, 23:07

```
 1. Ellen:    um [(0.7) well if Sophie or (0.3) say um (1.2)]
 2. Boy:         [  ° ↑oh:    oo ( . )   oh: oh   oo °  ]
 3. Ellen:    Sophie or Saskia (0.9) stole the money
 4.           [(0.6) um:      ] (1.6) I wouldn't really (0.6)
 5. Boy?:     [(°xxx°)        ]
 6. Girl:     °care°
 7. Ellen:    no yeah I wouldn't really mind because (0.8)
 8.           I dunno [it seems weird to me that (0.4) someone would
 9. Boy?:             [°( x )°
10. Ellen:    stop being (1.3)
11.           I [(suppose) ]
12. Teacher:    [would it) ]
13. Ellen:    because I'm such good friends with them that (1.0) y'just
14. Girl?:    you would try not [to be but you [don't
15. Ellen:                      [it-          [so I wouldn't
16. Teacher:                                  [so if: SOmebody stole
```

```
17.               some money off you      [(1.2)
18. Boy:                                  [°(hot cross [x)°
19. Teacher:                              [you wouldn't mind?
20. Ellen:    no [: not if they stole [off me
21. (???):    [(                 )
22. ?:        [(                 )
23. Teacher:                     [ SH sh sh ] shh
24. Ellen:    but um [(1.6) um (if) they stole off someone
25. Boy:              [°((barely audible whispering through to line
26.           30))°
27. Ellen:    I know it (0.8) I wouldn't [think-
28. Teacher:                             [if they stole off somebody
29.           else you mean
30. Ellen:    yeah
31. Teacher:  right
32. Ellen:    I wouldn't (0.4) stop being their friend
33.           but I (1.0) wouldn't exactly go oh]=
34. Boy:      ° ((whispering from line 23)) °    ]
35. Ellen:    =[that's (really good)
36. Boy?:     [HEY look after my bike? [°(kind of thing)°
37. Teacher:                           [ right yeah I see]
38. (???):                             [(            )]
39. Ellen:                             [ (xxx)         ]
40.           and also] [um
41. Teacher:           [oh ↑no::↓
```

In this extract, Ellen, who currently holds the floor as ratified speaker, begins by constructing a hypothetical scenario, relating the problem to her own set of good friends, 'well if say Sophie or Saskia stole the money' (lines 1–3). At the end of her turn she pauses, apparently searching for the word she wants, 'I wouldn't really (0.6)', and another pupil offers a candidate completion for her utterance, 'care'. Ellen accepts this by modifying it slightly, repeating her utterance but using her own word, 'no yeah I wouldn't really <u>mind</u>'. This is a new opinion in the discussion (and a controversial one compared to those given so far) which she goes on to justify (line 8). The teacher responds to this justification with, 'would it' (line 12), but by now other class members are beginning to contribute (line 9 and again in line 13). Here, as Ellen hesitates in her search to find the right words to make her point, another girl spontaneously offers a supporting clarification of her position, 'you would try to be but . . .'. It is however the teacher who takes up the role of offering a formulation of Ellen's position:

```
So if somebody stole some money off you you wouldn't mind?
```

This question prompts several responses, and is treated as 'open' to the floor. Ellen responds, but so do others in overlap with her (see lines 20, 21 and 22). The floor has by this stage become much more multi-party, and it is at this point that the teacher produces a sanctioning series of 'sh's' (line 23). Once the teacher has re-established space for Ellen to continue her role as current speaker, she is able to pursue her argument (from line 24). The teacher again clarifies the point she is making, 'if they stole off somebody else you mean' (line 28). This clarification is accepted, and Ellen moves into the closing stages of her turn with a constrastive utterance, 'I wouldn't stop being their friend, but I wouldn't exactly go (oh that's really good)'. The introduction of some direct speech here is a recurrent resource that the pupils use in the discursive development of their opinions,[9] bringing themselves into the hypothetical scenario they are constructing with a self quote:

```
I wouldn't exactly go 'oh that's really good'
```

What happens next is a further instance of candidate utterance completion by another pupil. Just when Ellen says 'go', a boy simultaneously offers an alternative possible self-quote:

```
HEY look after my bike
```

The placing of this utterance here displays very clearly that this pupil has not only been attending closely to the argument being made, but also that he has understood precisely its practical implications – the position this would put two friends in. The issue is not just disapproval of a friend's actions, but the consequent lack of the trust that would normatively hold between good friends – a friend is someone you could safely leave your bike with.

The three turns taken at lines 6, 14 and 36 by speakers other than Ellen, who officially has the right to the floor in this sequence, are ratified contributions in that they are tightly tied to the development of the main speaker's argument; they are linked to the preceding utterance both coherently in terms of the topic, and cohesively in terms of structure, offering respectively a candidate word to complete a turn, a candidate clarification and a candidate piece of direct speech relevant to the hypothetical scenario being built up. As such, they are not commented on as interruptive by either teacher or pupil, and thus are accepted as legitimate contributions to the point that is being made. However, when there are too many pupils talking simultaneously (lines 21 and 22, and later lines 38 and 39), and no one speaker can be heard above all the rest, then this is dealt with differently by the teacher, who now goes 'shhh'. The 'oh no' (line 41) which ends this segment of the discussion is ambiguous; it may be functioning as a comment on the continuing 'noise' in the previous two lines, but it may be due some incident with the tape (the transition to the next speaker here seems less fluent than preceding ones).

CONCLUSIONS

The classroom discussion seems then to be one kind of activity type where there is much more variation in the participatory structure compared to the 'instructional' discourse patterns of interaction in other kind of classroom talk I described at the beginning of this chapter. We have seen from the evidence in these data that the pupils' initial participation on a one-at-a-time basis becomes gradually less teacher regulated, and that the children move into a much more collaborative floor structure

(Edelsky, 1981) as the discussion develops. This means that the children are producing collaborative contributions which result in the successful construction of the discussion as a multi-party event. In so doing they widen the participation framework from one in which the teacher is primary opinion elicitor and opinion receiver and a designated pupil is opinion producer, to one in which many more pupils are involved in multiple participant roles as speakers, recipients and active collaborators in the on-going production of opinions.

The ratio of one-to-many in a teaching situation is clearly very different to the other contexts for institutional talk in the preceding analyses, which have been dialogic (in the case of the interview data) or where there is only one participant occupying a less powerful institutional role (as we saw in the discussion of calls to the phone-in of chapter 4 and the police interview of chapter 3). Although teachers may nominally occupy a role in the classroom which is institutionally inscribed as powerful, in practice this role can be very effectively resisted and challenged by pupils and made difficult to sustain in a disruptive classroom where class members may be more concerned with displaying unco-operative strategies. In these data, although the teacher can still be seen to retain a 'controlling' role in the speech event (distributing opinion-giving turns, nominating speakers and, when necessary, restoring a 'too-many-at-a-time' situation back to the 'one-at-a-time' norm of a discussion as a classroom activity), the children themselves display their involvement in constituting this activity as an institutional occasion by taking up appropriate and relevant positions as collaborative contributors to a jointly developing floor. While there are inevitably moments where too many pupils are talking at once, these are relatively few compared to the overall sense of orderly, collective participation in building a classroom discussion. And, when one pupil does not participate in this way, the others give clear indications that this lack of participation is inappropriate. In this kind of context for talk it is quite acceptable to say you are not sure, or to construct your opinion as an ongoing matter, but it is not acceptable to display inattention and to say you don't know.

So, although control of the talk can certainly be seen to be in some respects in the hands of the teacher, in many instances it can also be observed in the hands of the pupils. Through their increasingly active participation, and through the design of their contributions to the talk, they play a collaborative role in shaping the discussion as an orderly event within its institutional context.

NOTES

1. From this study Sinclair and Coulthard (1975) derived the interactional model of 'exchange structure' in discourse, a model intended to describe the rules and units of language use above the traditional unit of grammatical analysis, the clause, or sentence.
2. Sinclair and Coulthard comment on a lesson in their data where a teacher who consistently witheld feedback in order to suggest that there are not always right answers 'reduced the children to silence – they cannot see the point of his questions' (1975: 51).
3. The classroom is by no means the only context where this type of display questioning takes place; the same type of asymmetry can often be observed in adult/child interaction at home as well as in schools. A similar, although not identical format, is also found in

interviews where interviewees are required to display their knowledge and competence which is then assessed by the interviewers (cf. Gumperz, 1982b).

4. My thanks to colleagues at Roehampton Institute for these data.

5. When this is not the case, so-called 'free' schools (like Summerhill in Britain where the organisation and structure of the learning agenda is in the hands of the pupils) are often subjected to media scrutiny and inspectoral criticism (*Independent*, March 2000).

6. Manke's notion of an agreed agenda of co-operation in the classroom which shapes the power relations within that environment is based on McDermott and Tylbor's (1986) work on colluded-in agendas in interaction.

7. To preserve anonymity, the names of all schools have been changed.

8. As I discussed in chapter 4, Hutchby (1999) has noticed this phenomenon in callers' first turns in talk radio. It seems it may be more generalisable as a discourse feature in relation to how people take up the floor when publicly called upon to speak.

9. This extract is taken from a larger corpus of discussion talk.

7

◆

POWER AND INSTITUTIONAL INTERACTION: SOME CONCLUSIONS

This final chapter will be a short one, where I reassemble some of the analytic questions and methodological issues that have arisen during the course of the book about language, power and institutional interaction, and the ways that they interconnect. My starting point for an analysis of power in talk was to identify the need for closer attention to the micro-interactional details and participatory frameworks of talk in institutional settings, while remaining sensitive to the social and institutional identities of the participants. Through the analyses of some empirical data, I set out to show that the relationship between power and talk in institutional interaction cannot be accounted for simply in terms of pre-existing social relations of power which determine institutional discursive structures, but that neither can it be accounted for in isolation from those relations. In the series of case studies presented here, I have explored the ways in which the institutional and discursive identities of a range of different participants in various institutional settings, from a police interview room to a school classroom, are consequential for the kind of talk that gets done in those settings.

TALK AND ASYMMETRY

In the course of this exploration, I have stretched the theoretical notion of asymmetry from its conventional usage in conversation analysis, as a way of describing the structural organisation of talk in terms of how different types of turns are distributed between participants, to encompass a broader contextual notion of asymmetry that is closer to the concerns traditionally associated with critical discourse analysis: that of asymmetrical discursive roles and social, or institutional identities. In so doing, my purpose has been to relate three important analytic foci: the discursive identities set up during the talk event (for example, questioner, formulator or opinion-giver), the institutional identities of participants inscribed in that event (for example phone-in host, interviewee or school pupil) and the variable accessibility of different turn-types and discursive resources to those participants. So it is possible to see, on one level, that what an interviewer does is ask questions, and that asking questions can be a powerful discursive resource, because questions generally require answers. But it is also possible to see, on another level, what happens when questions are asked by participants with different institutional identities, and how those questions are dealt with by co-participants. One of the central arguments I have developed here is based on the now well-established tenet in CA that turn taking in institutional contexts is frequently distributed along quite structured lines, in terms of who occupies particular types of turns and interactional positions. From that basis, I have described how from within those interactional positions, speakers are able to access a range of discursive resources to take discursive actions, and I have shown that the upshot of those actions is to a significant extent shaped by a participant's current institutional identity. Thus, although it may be open to any participant to ask a question in response to a prior turn, a further asymmetry emerges between those participants who are under some obligation to answer questions, and those who are not, such as we saw in the police interview data.

A key element in the approach I have taken in this book is that power relations in interaction are not necessarily fixed, predetermined states of affairs, but are constantly shifting and being redefined between participants on a very local level. These shifts can be observed by looking at the participatory framework and structural organisation of the talk (typically, who gets which turns in a pre-allocated system), the changes in that structure (who manages to get access to a particular type of turn) and how those changes are dealt with by participants as they occur. So for example in chapter 2, we saw how the organisation of calls to a radio phone-in resulted in an attenuation of the caller's potentially powerful discursive role as questioner, the kind of resources some callers used to access that role, and the strategies that were available to the host for restoring the institutional order. In the interview data in chapter 3, interviewers' access to a 'formulating' receipt turn positions them in a potentially powerful interactional role, since it enables them to exercise a certain amount of control over the direction of the talk in terms of what kind of action will come next, as well as in terms of establishing gist, and determining emerging meanings in the talk. Interviewees consequently find strategies for resisting this control, as was shown in the analysis of responses to interviewer formulating turns. In the classroom data, the asymmetrical arrangement of teacher as opinion elicitor, and pupils and opinion givers in the discussion gradually breaks down as more and more pupils self select to speak and contribute to the talk without prior nomination by the teacher. It is only when the multi-party talk becomes unmanageable within the context of a discussion that the teacher re-asserts her role as regulator, and makes calls to order which restore one-at-a-time talk.

In all these cases, then, I have not measured interactional power in quantitative terms, by how much space there is to talk in, who occupies that space, and the means by which they get to occupy it. Neither have I considered the question of what gets talked about, whose topics get taken up, and whose do not. Instead, I have taken another approach, one in which power relations can be analysed on a very local discursive level. In this way, power in talk can be observed emerging at the interface between participants' current institutional identity, and the kind of turns this identity conventionally gives them access to, and what actually occurs when they move into other types of turns. Central to this approach is the view that although the same array of discursive strategies and resources may arguably be available to all the participants in institutional settings, how effectively those resources may be used is bound up with both the structural constraints of the talk and the institutional identities of the participants.

TALK AND INSTITUTIONAL SETTINGS

In the introductory chapter of this book I also raised the question of what counts as institutional discourse, and the various ways in which it has been delimited and described within the framework of discourse and conversation analysis. I suggested that the very concept of 'institutional' talk is problematic, and that much of the talk that goes on in what would typically be regarded as institutional settings may be highly conversational in nature. There is a tendency in the literature to conceive of 'institutional' and 'ordinary' settings for conversation as distinct categories; for example, Maynard (1992) observed that in some ways talk that takes place in institutional settings is 'continuous with that in ordinary life'. Setting the boundaries between what counts as institutional and what counts as ordinary is equally problematic if one considers social groupings or communities such as the family as institutional, a position upheld by most feminist discourse analysts.

Nevertheless, despite these reservations, there are particular types of talk which seem to be recognisable as inherently institutional in nature, in so far as they are closely associated with the contexts in which they occur. The examples of talk I have included from my data corpus in this book all fall into this category – on a very basic, commonsense level, it is hard to conceive of them as talk events occurring outside of those specific contexts (although this does not mean that the discursive actions through which they are constituted could not occur elsewhere). While the distinction between what might be thought of as institutional and non-institutional discourse remains blurred, particularly in relation to spoken discourse, in the data analysed in chapters 3–6 (a police interview, a radio phone-in, a news interview and a class discussion), the talk displays all of the characteristics listed at the beginning of chapter 1. Participants in all these talk events have institutional identities which are linked structurally and asymmetrically to access different types of turns and discursive identities: they are pupils, police officers, callers, complainants, interviewers. There is a corresponding asymmetry in speaker rights and obligations, and in the relative consequences and outcomes of discursive resources speakers deploy.

There are very few moments where the talk approaches being 'conversational', and again I treat this term with caution. One of the rare occasions which springs to mind in the data is in chapter 4, a sequence in the phone-in data where a fairly informal exchange develops between a caller and the host on the subject of Margaret Thatcher and a video. During this call, however, the conventional framework of roles and turn positions of host and caller are still maintained, and it is simply the topic and its informal design that produces a more conversational keying of this sequence. Even in the multi-party classroom discussion when the more clearly restricted institutional pattern – teacher selecting next speaker, pupil producing an opinion, followed by teacher acceptance or evaluation – gives way to more conversational norms of next speaker selection, the talk produced by the children in this context nevertheless displays their clear orientation to the institutional event they are constructing, and their role in that event, through their forms of participation and interaction.

POWER IN TALK

In this discussion of talk and power in institutional discourse, I have pursued three main strands of analysis. I have looked at aspects of the linguistic choices speakers make in designing their utterances, I have attended to the turn-by-turn detail of talk as situated interaction, and I have considered the consequences of asymmetrical status in participants' institutional identities. In doing so, I have tried to make the best use of some different methodological frameworks, drawing on the analytic tools of conversation analysis, Goffman's concepts of interactional sociolinguistics and Foucault's theoretical model of the 'web' of power.

The rationale for this multi-layered approach, as I discuss in chapter 2, is one which is shared by other analysts who are concerned to encourage the links between what are frequently seen as incompatible positions (Miller, 1997). It is increasingly being argued that communication between the diverse fields of study which focus on situated discourse (in particular the ethnography of speaking, conversation analysis and work based on Gumperz's (1982b) notions of contextualisation) will strengthen those individual fields. In their account of how context is currently being conceptualised in research into language and social interaction, Goodwin and Duranti (1992) show how different perspectives in the study of talk offer a productive range of ways forward in the analysis of context as 'an interactively constituted mode of praxis' (1992: 9).

In the analyses of institutionally situated talk presented here, my aim has been to contribute to that communication between research traditions, and to bring some of the issues that are frequently aired during the ongoing theoretical debates (Billig, 1999; Schegloff, 1999) into a more empirical domain. I do this by focusing closely on the detail of naturally occurring interaction as it is produced in four different institutional settings, and by examining the reflexive relationship between the social status and identity of participants in that setting, and their talk.

In the course of these analyses I have identified the discursive actions and turn positions with which and from which it is possible to do powerful things. From this very local, moment-by-moment interactional perspective, power can be construed as one participant's ability to affect or influence what the next participant does in the next turn. But within institutional contexts for talk, I have argued that these discursive actions and turn positions function as powerful in relation to other contextual features of role and identity. As we have seen at various points in many examples from the data, asking a question, or reformulating the gist of a participant's utterance in a receipt turn, or simply remaining silent, can all be powerfully situated discursive actions; but the key to how those actions are received and attended to in the talk is the relative institutional identity and status of the participants.

The data I have analysed here represent some very different types of institutional interaction, and there is a wide variation in the degree of asymmetrical relations which exist between participants in terms of their social and institutional identities. In the interview between the woman making a complaint of rape and the police officers the asymmetries are multiple, and this shows through in the talk on many different levels, not simply in the turn-taking patterns but also in the framework for interaction as well as on the representational level of competing versions of events. Power in this encounter is visibly and hearably out in the open. In the radio phone-in programme, again the asymmetrical relationships between host, guest and callers was marked, particularly in view of the relative age and social status of the participants. The power relations in this case study were located more specifically in the participatory framework and restricted access to particular types of turns. Once that framework was broken, it became possible for callers to occupy different turn positions and consequently to deploy a greater range of discursive resources within those turns. In the news interviews, on the other hand, the asymmetries between participants were much less marked, and this enabled us to see more clearly how strategies of resistance to potentially powerful discursive actions were engaged and mobilised in the talk. For professional interviewers and professional interviewees, such as politicians, negotiating the space to say what you have to say is crucially a matter of dealing with what has just occurred in the prior turn. Finally, in the classroom discussion data, the asymmetrical relations that are generally taken to hold between teacher and pupils were not so visible. The teacher was certainly occupying her institutional role in the discussion as distributor of opinion-giving speaker turns and occasional regulator of the talk to restore order. However, this regulatory role was also occasionally taken up by pupils, and, more generally, it was their collaborative participation in the talk that played a central part in holding the talk to its conventional, orderly institutional norms.

To return to Foucault's conceptualisation of power as an intricate web of social and discursive relations, as a 'productive network' within which people are always both the agents of power and affected by it, then the social practice of language in interaction is a primary site where those relations can be seen to be constructed and resisted. Foucault has also claimed that where there is power there will be resistance to power, and, in institutional interaction, both the location of power and the resistance to it can be observed by tracking these shifts in speaker roles and discursive identities as they are played out in the action of the ongoing talk. This then has been my main objective in the book, to look at power not as it might be owned, possessed or unequally distributed between social agents, but as a locally produced and analysable phenomenon in the social interaction between participants in talk in institutional settings.

BIBLIOGRAPHY

———— ◆ ————

Althusser, L. 1971 *Lenin and Philosophy and Other Essays*. London: New Left Books.

Atkinson, J.M. and Drew, P. 1979 *Order in Court: The Organisation of Verbal Interaction in Judicial Settings*. London: Macmillan.

Atkinson, J.M. and Heritage, J. 1984 *Structures of Social Action*. Cambridge: Cambridge University Press.

Austin, J. 1962 *How to Do Things with Words*. Oxford: Clarendon Press.

Bakhtin, M. 1981 *The Dialogical Imagination* (ed. M. Holquist, trans. C. Emerson and M. Holquist). Austin: University of Texas Press.

Bakhtin, M. 1986 *Speech Genres and Other Late Essays* (ed. C. Emerson and M. Holquist, trans. V.W. McGee). Austin: University of Texas Press.

Billig, M. 1999 Whose terms? Whose ordinariness? Rhetoric and ideology in conversation analysis. *Discourse and Society*, 10(4): 543–58.

Black, M. and Coward, R. 1981 Linguistic, social and sexual relations: a review of Dale Spender's 'Man-made Language'. *Screen Education*, 39: 69–85.

Blum Kulka, S. 1997 *Dinner Talk: Cultural Patterns of Sociability and Socialization in Family Discourse*. Mahwah, NJ: Lawrence Erlbaum.

Boden, D. 1994 *The Business of Talk: Organisations in Action*. Cambridge: Polity.

Boden, D. and Zimmerman, D. 1991 *Talk and Social Structure. Studies in Ethnomethodology and Conversation Analysis*. Cambridge: Polity.

Bourdieu, P. 1992 *Language and Symbolic Power*. Cambridge: Polity Press.

Brown, P. and Levinson, S. 1987 *Politeness: Some Universals in Language Usage*. Cambridge: Cambridge University Press.

Cameron, D. 1985 *Feminism and Linguistic Theory*. London: Macmillan.

Cameron, D. 1997 Theoretical debates in feminist linguistics. In R. Wodak (ed.) *Gender and Discourse*. London: Sage, pp. 21–36.

Cameron, D., McAlinden, F. and O'Leary, K. 1989 Lakoff in context: the social and linguistic function of tag questions. In D. Cameron and J. Coates (eds) *Women in Their Speech Communities*. London: Longman, pp. 74–93.

Chilton, P. (ed.) 1985 *Language and the Nuclear Arms Debate: Nukespeak Today*. London: Frances Pinter.

Chouliaraki, L. 1996 Regulative practices in a 'progressivist' classroom: 'good habits' as a 'disciplinary technology'. *Language and Education*, 10(2 and 3): 103–18.

Clayman, S. 1989 The production of punctuality: social interaction, temporal organization and social structure. *American Journal of Sociology*, 95: 659–91.

Clayman, S. 1992 Footing in the achievement of neutrality: the case of news-interview discourse. In P. Drew and J. Heritage (eds) *Talk at Work: Interaction in Institutional Settings*. Cambridge: Cambridge University Press, pp. 163–98.

Clegg, S. 1993 Narrative, power and social theory. In D.K. Mumby (ed.) *Narrative and Social Control: Critical Perspectives*. London: Sage, pp. 15–45.

Coates, J. 1994 No gap lots of overlap: turn-taking patterns in the talk of women friends. In D. Graddol, J. Maybin and B. Stierer (eds) *Researching Language and Literacy in Social Context*. Clevedon, Avon: Multilingual Matters, pp. 177–92.

Coates, J. 1996 *Women Talk: Conversation between Women Friends*. Oxford: Blackwell.

Conley, J. and O'Barr, W. 1990 Rules versus relationships in small claims disputes. In A. Grimshaw (ed.) *Conflict Talk*. Cambridge: Cambridge University Press, pp. 178–96.

Crystal, D. 1987 *The Cambridge Encylopedia of Language*. Cambridge: Cambridge University Press.

Dahl, R. 1961 *Who Governs? Democracy and Power in an American City*. New Haven, CT: Yale University Press.

DeFrancisco, V. 1991 The sounds of silence: how men silence women in marital relations. *Discourse and Society*, 2(4): 413–24.

Diamond, J. 1996 *Status and Power in Verbal Interaction: A Study of Discourse in a Close-knit Social Network*. Pragmatics and Beyond, New Series 40. Amsterdam/Philadelphia: John Benjamins.

Drew, P. 1981 Adults' corrections of children's mistakes: a response to Wells and Montgomery. In P. French and M. Maclure (eds) *Adult Child Conversation*. London: Croom Helm, pp. 244–67.

Drew, P. 1992 Contested evidence in courtroom cross-examinations: the case of a trial for rape. In P. Drew and J. Heritage (eds), pp. 470–520.

Drew, P. forthcoming 2001 Comparative analysis of talk-in-interaction in different institutional settings: a sketch. In G. Lebaron and J. Mandelbaum (eds) *Excavating the Taken for Granted: Essays in Language and Social Interaction*. Mahwah, NJ: Erlbaum.

Drew, P. and Heritage, J. 1992a *Talk at Work: Interaction in Institutional Settings*. Cambridge: Cambridge University Press.

Drew, P. and Heritage, J. 1992b Analyzing talk at work: an introduction. In P. Drew and J. Heritage (eds) 1992a, pp. 3–65.

Eckert, P. and McConnell-Ginet, S. 1992. Communities of practice: where language, gender and power all live. In K. Hall, M. Bucholz and B. Moonwomon (eds) *Locating Power: Proceedings of the Second Berkeley Women and Language Conference, Vol. I*. Berkeley, CA: Berkeley Women and Language Group, University of California, Berkeley, pp. 89–99.

Edelsky, C. 1981 Who's got the floor? *Language in Society*, 10: 383–421.

Edwards, A.D. and Westgate, D.P.G. 1992 *Investigating Classroom Talk* (2nd edn). London: Falmer Press.

Ehrlich, S. 1998 The discursive reconstruction of sexual consent. *Discourse and Society*, 9(2): 149–71.

Fairclough, N. 1989 *Language and Power*. London: Longman.

Fairclough, N. 1992 *Discourse and Social Change*. Cambridge: Polity Press.

Fairclough, N. 1995 *Critical Discourse Analysis: The Critical Study of Language*. Harlow, Essex: Longman.

Fisher, E. 1993 Distinctive features of pupil–pupil classroom talk and their relationship to learning: how discursive exploration might be encouraged. *Language and Education*, 7(4): 239–57.

Fishman, P. 1983 Interaction: the work women do. In B. Thorne, C. Kramerae and N. Henley (eds) *Language, Gender and Society*. Rowley, MA: Newbury House, pp. 89–102.

Foucault, M. 1972 *The Archaeology of Knowledge* (trans. A.M. Sheridan Smith). London: Tavistock.

Foucault, M. 1977 *Discipline and Punish* (trans. A. Sheridan). New York: Pantheon.

Foucault, M. 1980 *Power/Knowledge* (trans. C. Gordon). New York: Pantheon.

Fowler, R., Hodge, R., Kress, G. and Trew, T. 1979 *Language as Control*. London: Routledge.

Fowler, R. 1991 *Language in the News*. London: Routledge.

French, P. and MacLure, M. (eds) 1981 *Adult Child Conversation*. London: Croom Helm.

Gal, S. 1992 Language, gender and power: an anthroplogical view. In K. Hall, M. Bucholz and B. Moonwomon (eds) *Locating Power: Proceedings of the Second Berkeley Women and Language Conference, Vol I*. Berkeley, CA: Berkeley Women and Language Group, University of California, Berkeley, pp. 153–61.

Garton, G., Tolson, A. and Montgomery, M. 1991 Ideology, scripts and metaphors in the public sphere of a general election. In P. Scannell (ed.), pp. 100–18.

Goffman, E. 1981 *Forms of Talk*. Oxford: Blackwell.

Goffman, E. 1983 The interaction order. *American Sociological Review*, 48: 1–17.

Goldberg, J. 1990 Interrupting the discourse on interruptions: an analysis in terms of relationally neutral, power- and rapport-oriented acts. *Journal of Pragmatics*, 14: 883–903.

Goodwin, C. and Duranti, A. (eds) 1992 *Rethinking Context: Language as an Interactive Phenomenon*. Cambridge: Cambridge University Press.

Goodwin, C. and Harness Goodwin, M. 1990 Interstitial argument. In A. Grimshaw (ed.) *Conflict Talk*. Cambridge: Cambridge University Press, pp. 85–117.

Goodwin, M. 1990 *He-Said-She-Said: Talk as Social Organization among Black Children*. Bloomington and Indianapolis: Indiana University Press.

Goodwin, M. 1992 Orchestrating participation in events: Powerful talk among African American girls. In K. Hall, M. Bucholtz and B. Moonwomon (eds), pp. 182–96.

Greatbach, D. 1986 Aspects of topical organisation in news interviews: the use of agenda shifting procedures by interviewees. *Media Culture and Society*, **8**(4): 441–55.

Greatbach, D. 1988 A turntaking system for British news interviews. *Language in Society*, 17: 401–30.

Greatbach, D. 1993 On the management of disagreement between news interviewees. In P. Drew and J. Heritage (eds), pp. 268–301.

Grimshaw, A. (ed.) 1990 *Conflict Talk: Sociolinguistic Investigations of Arguments in Conversations*. Cambridge: Cambridge University Press.

Gumperz, J. 1982a *Language and Social Identity*. Cambridge: Cambridge University Press.

Gumperz, J. 1982b *Discourse Strategies*. Cambridge: Cambridge University Press.

Gwyn, R. 1998 Review of Silverman 1997. *Journal of Sociolinguistics* 2(1): 130–3.

Habermas, J. 1984 *Theory of Communicative Action, Vol. 1* (trans T. McCarthy). London: Heinemann.

Hall, S. 1982 The rediscovery of ideology: the return of the repressed in media studies. In M. Gurevitch, M. Curran and J. Woollacott (eds) *Culture, Society and the Media*. London: Methuen, pp. 56–90.

Halliday, M.A.K. 1978 *Language as a Social Semiotic*. London: Edward Arnold.

Halliday, M.A.K. 1985 *An Introduction to Functional Grammar*. London: Arnold.

Harris, S. 1984 Questions as a mode of control in magistrates' courts. *International Journal of the Sociology of Language*, 49: 5–27.

Harris, S. 1991 Evasive action: politicians and political interviews. In P. Scannell (ed.) *Broadcast Talk*. London: Sage, pp. 76–99.

Harris, S. 1995 Pragmatics and power. *Journal of Pragmatics*, 23: 117–35.

Heritage, J. 1984 *Garfinkel and Ethnomethodology*. Cambridge: Polity Press.

Heritage, J. 1985 Analysing news interviews. In T. Van Dijk (ed.) *Handbook of Discourse Analysis, Vol. 3*. London: Academic Press, pp. 95–117.

Heritage, J. and Greatbach, D. 1991 On the institutional character of institutional talk: the case of news interviews. In D. Boden and D. Zimmerman (eds) *Talk and Social Structure.* Cambridge: Polity Press, pp. 93–137.

Heritage, J. and Watson, D.R. 1979 Formulations as conversational objects. In G. Psathas (ed.) *Everyday Language: Studies in Ethnomethodology.* New York: Irvington, pp. 123–62.

Herring, S., Johnson, D. and DiBenedetto, T. 1998 Participation in electronic discourse in a 'feminist' field. In J. Coates (ed.) *Language and Gender: A Reader.* Oxford: Blackwell, pp. 197–210.

Hodge, R. and Kress, G. 1993 *Language as Ideology* (2nd edn). London: Routledge.

Hopper, R. 1992 *Telephone Conversation.* Bloomington, IN: Indiana University Press.

Houtkoop-Steenstra, H. 1991 Opening sequences in Dutch telephone conversations. In D. Boden and D. Zimmerman (eds), pp. 232–50.

Hutchby, I. 1992 Confrontation talk: Aspects of 'interruption' in argument sequences on talk radio. *Text,* 12(3): 343–71.

Hutchby, I. 1996a *Confrontation Talk: Arguments, Asymmetries and Power on Talk Radio.* Hillsdale, NJ: Lawrence Erlbaum.

Hutchby, I. 1996b Power in discourse: the case of arguments on a British talk radio show. *Discourse and Society,* 7(4): 481–97.

Hutchby, I. 1997 Building alignments in public debate: a case study from British TV. *Text,* 17(2): 161–79.

Hutchby, I. 1999 Frame attunement and footing in the organisation of talk radio openings. *Journal of Sociolinguistics,* 3(1): 41–63.

Jefferson, G. 1978 Sequential aspects of storytelling in conversation. In J. Schenkein (ed.) *Studies in the Organisation of Conversational Interaction.* New York: Free Press, pp. 219–48.

Jefferson, G. 1981 The abominable 'ne?': a working paper exploring the phenomenon of post-response pursuit of response. Occasional Paper 6, Department of Sociology, University of Manchester.

Jones, A. 1989 The cultural production of classroom practice. *British Journal of Sociology of Educataion,* 10: 19–31.

Kress, G. and Hodge, R. 1979 *Language as Ideology.* London: Routledge.

Labov, W. and Fanshel, D. 1977 *Therapeutic Discourse: Psychotherapy as Conversation.* New York: Academic Press.

Lakoff, R. 1975 *Language and Women's Place.* New York: Harper & Row.

Lerner, G. 1995 Turn design and the organisation of participation in instructional activities. *Discourse Processes,* 19: 111–31.

Levinson, S. 1983 *Pragmatics.* Cambridge: Cambridge University Press.

Levinson, S. 1988 Putting linguistics on a proper footing. In P. Drew and T. Wootton (eds) *Erving Goffman: Exploring the Interaction Order.* Cambridge: Polity Press, pp. 161–227.

Levinson, S. 1992 Activity types and language. In P. Drew and J. Heritage (eds), pp. 66–100.

Livingstone, S. and Lunt, P. 1994 *Talk on Television.* London: Routledge.

Lukes, S. 1974 *Power: A Radical View.* London: Macmillan.

MacDonnel, D. 1986 *Theories of Discourse.* Oxford: Blackwell.

McDermott, R.P. and Tylbor, H. 1986 On the necessity of collusion in conversation. In S. Fisher and A. Todd (eds) *Discourse and Institutional Authority: Medicine, Education and Law.* Norwood, NJ: Ablex, pp. 123–39.

McElhinny, B. 1997 Ideologies of public and Private Language in Sociolinguistics. In R. Wodak (ed.) *Gender and Discourse.* London: Sage, pp. 106–39.

McHoul, A. 1978 The organisation of turns at formal talk in the classroom. *Language in Society*, 7: 183–213.

Mandelbaum, D. 1949 *Selected Writings of Edward Sapir*. Berkeley, CA: University of California Press.

Manke, M. Phillips 1997 *Classroom Power Relations: Understanding Student–Teacher Interaction*. Mahwah, NJ: Lawrence Erlbaum.

Maynard, D. 1992 On clinicians co-implicating and recipient's perspective in the delivery of diagnostic news. In P. Drew and J. Heritage (eds), pp. 331–58.

Mehan, H. 1991 The school's work of sorting students. In D. Boden and D. Zimmerman (eds), pp. 71–90.

Miller, G. 1997 Bridging. In D. Silverman (ed.) *Qualitative Research: Theory, Method and Practice*. London: Sage, pp. 24–44.

Minsky, M. 1985 A framework for representing knowledge. In R.J. Brachman and H.J. Levesque (eds) *Readings in Knowledge Representation*. Los Altos, CA: Morgan Kaufmann, pp. 245–62.

Mishler, E. 1984 *The Discourse of Medicine: Dialectics of Medical Interviews*. Norwood, NJ: Ablex.

Montgomery, M. 1986a *An Introduction to Language and Society*. London: Methuen.

Montgomery, M. 1986b DJ talk. *Media Culture and Society*, 8(4): 421–40.

Nelson, M.W. (1988, 1998) Women's ways: interactive patterns in predominantly female research teams. In J. Coates (ed.) *Language and Gender: A Reader*. Oxford: Blackwell, pp. 354–72.

O'Barr, W. and Atkins, B. 1980 'Women's language' or 'Powerless language'. In S. McConnell-Ginet, R. Borker and C. Marrett (eds) *Women and Language in Literature and Society*. New York: Praeger, pp. 93–110.

Ochs, E. 1979 Planned and unplanned discourse. In T. Givòn (ed.) *Syntax and Semantics 12: Discourse and Syntax*. New York: Academic Press, pp. 51–80.

Ochs, E. and Taylor, C. 1992. Family narrative as political activity. *Discourse and Society*, 3(3): 301–40.

Pateman, T. 1980 *Language, Truth and Politics* (2nd edn). Lewes, Sussex: Jean Strand.

Pecheux, M. 1982 *Language, Semantics and Ideology* (trans. H. Nagpal). London: Macmillan.

Pomerantz, A. 1984 Agreeing and disagreeing with assessments: some features of preferred/dispreferred turn shapes. In J.M. Atkinson and J. Heritage (eds), pp. 79–112.

Pomerantz, A. 1989 Epilogue. *Western Journal of Speech Communication*, 53: 242–46.

Sacks, H. 1978 Some technical considerations of a dirty joke. In J. Schenkein (ed.) *Studies in the Organisation of Conversational Interaction*. New York: Academic Press, pp. 249–69.

Sacks, H. 1995 *Lectures on Conversation Vols I and II* (ed. G. Jefferson). Oxford: Blackwell.

Sacks, H., Schegloff, E. and Jefferson, G. 1974 A simplest systematics for the organisation of turn-taking in conversation. *Language*, 50(4): 696–735.

Sattel, J. 1983 Men, inexpressiveness and power. In B. Thorne, C. Kramerae and N. Henley (eds) *Language Gender and Society*, Rowley, MA: Newbury House, pp. 118–24.

de Saussure, F. 1959 *Course in General Linguistics* (trans. W. Baskin). New York: McGraw Hill.

Scannell, P. (ed.) 1991 *Broadcast Talk*. London: Sage.

Scannell, P. 1996 *Radio, Television and Modern Life*. Oxford: Blackwell.

Schegloff, E. 1972 Sequencing in conversational openings. In J. Gumperz and D. Hymes (eds) *Directions in Sociolinguistics*. New York: Holt, Reinhart & Wilson, pp. 346–80.

Bibliography

Schegloff, E. 1979 Identification and recognition in telephone conversation openings. In G. Psathas (ed.) *Everyday Language: Studies in Ethnomethodology*. New York: Ervington Press, pp. 23–78.

Schegloff, E. 1982 Discourse as an interactional achievement: some uses of 'uh huh' and other things that come between sentences. In *Analyzing Discourse: Text and Talk*. Washington DC: Georgetown University Press, pp. 71–93.

Schegloff, E. 1991 Reflections on talk and social structure. In D. Boden and D. Zimmerman (eds), pp. 44–70.

Schegloff, E. 1997 Whose text? Whose context? *Discourse and Society*, 8(2): 165–87.

Schegloff, E. 1999 'Schegloff's texts' as 'Billig's data': A critical reply. *Discourse and Society*, 10(4): 558–72.

Schegloff, E., Jefferson, G. and Sacks, H. 1977 The preference for self correction in the organisation of repair in conversation. *Language*, 53: 361–82.

Schiffrin, D. 1984. How a story says what it means and does. *Text*, 4(4): 313–46.

Scollon, R. and Scollon, S. 1981 *Narrative, Literacy and Face in Interethnic Communication*. Norwood, NJ: Ablex.

Shank, R. and Abelson, R.P. (1977) *Scripts, Plans, Goals and Understanding*. Hillsdale, NJ: Erlbaum.

Silverman, D. 1997 *Discourses of Counselling: HIV Counselling as Social Interaction*. London: Sage.

Simpson, P. 1993 *Language, Ideology and Point of View*. London: Routledge.

Sinclair, J. and Coulthard, M. 1975 *Towards an Analysis of Discourse: The English used by Teachers and Pupils*. Oxford: Oxford University Press.

Spender, D. 1980 *Man Made Language*. London: Routledge.

Tannen, D. 1992 *You Just Don't Understand: Women and Men in Conversation*. London: Virago Press.

Ten Have, P. 1991 Talk and institution: a reconsideration of the 'asymmetry' of doctor–patient interaction. In D. Boden and D. Zimmerman (eds), pp. 138–63.

Thornborrow, J. 1991 Orderly discourse and background knowledge. *Text*, 11(4): 581–606.

Thornborrow, J. 1997 Having their say: the function of stories in talk show discourse. *Text*, 17(2): 241–62.

Thornborrow, J. 2001 Questions, control and the organization of talk in calls to a radio phone-in. *Discourse Studies*, 3(1): 119–42.

Trew, T. 1979 What the papers say: linguistic variation and ideological difference. In R. Fowler *et al.* (eds), pp. 117–56.

Van Dijk, T.A. (ed.) 1985 *Discourse and Communication*. Berlin, New York: Walter de Gruyter.

Van Dijk, T.A. 1991 *Racism and the Press*. London: Routledge.

Van Dijk, T.A. 1993 *Elite Discourse and Racism*. Newbury Park, CA: Sage.

van Dijk, T.A. 1998 Opinions and ideologies in the press. In A. Bell and P. Garrett (eds) *Approaches to Media Discourse*. Oxford: Blackwell, pp. 21–63.

Wells, G. and Montgomery, M. 1981 Adult–child interaction at home and at school. In P. French and M. Maclure (eds) *Adult Child Conversation*. London: Croom Helm, pp. 210–41.

Wetherell, M. 1998 Positioning and interpretative repertoires: conversation analysis and post structuralism in dialogue. *Discourse and Society*, 9(3): 387–412.

Wodak, R. 1993 'We are dealing with people whose origins one can clearly tell just by looking': Critical discourse analysis and the study of neo-racism in contemporary Austria. *Discourse and Society*, 2(4) 225–48.

Wodak, R. 1996 The genesis of racist discourse in Austria since 1989. In C.C. Coulthard and M. Coulthard (eds) *Texts and Practices: Readings in Critical Discourse Analysis*. London: Routledge, pp. 107–28.

Zimmerman, D. and West, C. 1975 Sex roles, interruptions and silences in conversation. In B. Thorne and N. Henley (eds) *Language and Sex: Difference and Dominance*. Rowley, MA: Newbury House, pp. 105–29.

Zimmerman, D. 1992 The interactional organization of calls for emergency assistance. In P. Drew and J. Heritage (eds), pp. 418–69.

INDEX

——— ◆ ———